Modern Spirituality: An Anthology

Edited by John Garvey

Templegate Publishers
Springfield, Illinois

Modern Spirituality
An Anthology

ISBN 0-87243-162-2

Acknowledgements

Chapter 1 from: *The Way of Man* by Martin Buber © 1966, published by arrangement with Lyle Stuart.

Chapter 2 from: *Quest for God* by Abraham Joshua Heschel © 1954; renewed 1982, published with the permission of Charles Scribner's Sons.

Chapter 3 from: *Mixed Pasture* by Evelyn Underhill © 1933, Longmans Green.

Chapter 4 from: *Living Prayer* by Metropolitan Anthony Bloom © 1966, Templegate Publishers.

Chapter 5 from: *The Spiritual Father in Orthodox Christianity* by Kallistos Ware © 1974, by Cross Currents.

Chapter 6 from: *The Beatitudes: Soundings in Christian Traditions* by Simon Tugwell © 1980, Templegate Publishers.

Chapter 7 from: *The Eternal Year* by Karl Rahner, Helicon Press, Baltimore © 1964.

Chapter 8 from: *On the Invocation of the Name of Jesus* by Lev Gillet © 1949, Fellowship of Sts. Alban and Sergius.

Chapter 9 from: *Letters to Malcolm: Chiefly on Prayer* by C. S. Lewis © 1963, 1964 by the Estate of C. S. Lewis and/or C. S. Lewis, reprinted by permission of Harcourt Brace Jovanovich, Inc.

Chapter 10 from: *Heaven in Ordinarie* by Noel Dermot O'Donoghue © 1979, Templegate Publishers.

Chapter 11 from: *The Inner Eye of Love: Mysticism and Religion* by William Johnston © 1978, reprinted by permission of Harper & Row, Publishers, Inc.

Chapter 12 from: *Compassion* © 1982 by Donald P. McNeill, Douglas A. Morrison and Henri J. M. Nouwen, reprinted by permission of Doubleday & Co., Inc.

Chapter 13 from: *Cutting Through Spiritual Materialism* by Chögyam Trungpa © 1973, reprinted with permission of Shambhala Publications, Inc., Boulder, CO.

Chapter 14 from: *Zen and the Birds of Appetite* by Thomas Merton, © 1968 by the Abbey of Gethsemani, Inc., reprinted by permission of New Directions Publishing Corp.

Chapter 15 from: *Waiting for God* by Simone Weil, © 1951, renewal © 1979, reprinted by permission of G.P. Putnam's Sons.

Templegate Publishers
302 East Adams Street, P.O. Box 5152
Springfield, Illinois, 62705

Table of Contents

Introduction

There is a widespread assumption that spirituality is a personal and private concern, a matter of subjective taste, like collecting china. It must be made relevant to more "real" problems and concerns, which are the ones the secular understanding we all share defines for us: war and peace, poverty, the pursuit of power and influence, and so forth. And it is true that a spirituality which ignores the hungry is bankrupt. But the distinction which some would make between devotional belief and the social gospel, the playing of one off the other, is a false one. In his epistle, James tells us that our wars and conflicts start out in our hearts, in our disordered motives. (James 4, 1-3) And when one Orthodox monk was asked what a monk was, he said "A monk is someone who can weep for the whole world." The great spiritual traditions would all agree that many of the problems which the modern industrial nations have tended to categorize as political and economic have roots in the heart, which can be seen clearly only with attention and discipline. That discipline is what spirituality is concerned with.

The predominance of a secular point of view made spirituality appear as a separate concept. It is hard to imagine the use of a word like "spirituality" by Maximus the Confessor or one of the Fathers or Mothers of the Desert, who didn't think they were talking about a category called spirituality but rather about the way the souls of human beings work — about the most basic human truths; in other words, the ones we need to know and practice in order to become what we are meant to be.

But even though the Renaissance and later the Enlightenment made a major change in the way Westerners regarded the place of religious tradition, the tradition (or perhaps it would be better to say "traditions") continued as living facts in the lives of many people and many communities. There is not a radical difference between what is said here by Metropolitan Anthony Bloom and Lev Gillet and Kallistos Ware, for example, and what would have been said by any of the Desert Fathers or Gregory Palamas. What C. S. Lewis and Evelyn Underhill and Simon Tugwell say is not at some arms-length from what has been said by Brother Lawrence of the Resurrection or Catherine of Siena.

What is new is that people from different traditions are able to approach one another with an attitude which goes beyond the previous defensiveness. Christians have become aware of a Jewish heritage which has influenced everything from Christian liturgy and canon law to the most profound depths of Christian theology; many Jewish writers have dealt sensitively with the Jewishness of Jesus; and people whose religious heritage is Western have found Buddhist approaches to spirituality surprisingly helpful. The surprise comes in the recognition that many of the generalizations we had grown used to (for example, about Buddhism's agnostic or "non-theistic" aspects) said relatively little about Buddhism, and that the reality of Buddhist agnosticism about divinity has less to do with the rejection of God than with a radical criticism of the way the mind automatically makes things of ideas, and worships them. There is in Buddhism a radical approach to language and thought which could be seen as having something in common with the anti-idolatry of the prophets.

The life of Thomas Merton in some ways exemplifies the direction spirituality has taken in our time. Without abandoning his commitments to Cistercian monasticism within the Roman Catholic church, he was open to Eastern Orthodox spirituality, and in his last years he was increasingly influenced by Buddhism. He also insisted on the fact that genuine spirituality can not be detached from the struggles and pains of the world, but is a necessary precondition for seeing human suffering with any clarity.

Merton is also one of those writers — they seem to grow in number from the time of World War One until the present — who made it clear that contemplative spirituality was not a purely monastic concern. Books about meditation and prayer are read steadily by a primarily lay audience, or by men and women in active forms of ministry who have very little opportunity for monastic living. There is a renewed interest in the classics of Eastern and Western spirituality; new editions of *The Imitation of Christ, The Practice of the Presence of God, Revelations of Divine Love*, and *The Cloud of Unknowing* have appeared during the past few years.

The purpose of this anthology is to offer a sampling of some of the best modern spiritual writers. There is a range of emphases here; there are also several religious traditions represented, and this may require some explanation. Buber and Heschel are here because of the deep influence these two Jewish thinkers have had on modern

Introduction

Christian thought. Similarly, Simone Weil's influence is undeniable (the selection here may help to show why); although she was never baptized, she was a believer in Christianity who had a unique feeling for the universal nature of God's revelation. The presence of Chögyam Trungpa, a Buddhist, may require a little more explanation. The basic reason for his being here is quite personal: I find what he has to say about "spiritual materialism" very important. I think the readers of this anthology will find that it applies to the spirituality of any tradition, and that it is an important contribution. The other reason is that Trungpa in some ways reveals from the Buddhist perspective the direction which Merton revealed from a Christian perspective. Chögyam Trungpa's Naropa Institute has played an important role in the dialogue between Buddhism and the religions of the West. It is a dialogue which continues, and which many Christians find helpful.

The remaining contributors are Catholic, Orthodox, and Anglican. The topics covered include the techniques involved in prayer, the increasingly popular "prayer of the heart," the need for spiritual direction, the relationship between prayer and activism, and many other important facets of the life of prayer. I hope other readers will find the authors represented here as helpful as I have.

I don't pretend to have made an absolutely inclusive sweep here. The emphasis is clearly on Christian spirituality; that is the tradition I am most familiar with, and the one in which I believe. I am conscious that there are many other writers who could be included in an anthology of modern spirituality. The good thing about our situation is that there is so much that is good to choose from, new writing as well as fine editions of the classics of spirituality, that no one is ever likely to run dry.

— John Garvey

Heart Searching and the Particular Way

Martin Buber

Martin Buber (1878-1965) is one of the best known modern religious writers. His influence on Christians was at least as great as it was on his fellow Jews. He was a philosopher, editor, writer, translator of the Bible (with Franz Rosenzweig), and an ardent Zionist who was deeply concerned with the rights of Arabs in Israel. Buber was perhaps known best for I and Thou *and for his many studies of Hasidism. Here Buber offers some considerations which are at the foundation of any honest spirituality.*

I. Heart-Searching

Rabbi Shneur Zalman, The Rav[1] of Northern White Russia (died 1813), was put in jail in Petersburg, because the mitnagdim[2] had denounced his principles and his way of living to the government. He was awaiting trial when the chief of the gendarmes entered his cell. The majestic and quiet face of the rav, who was so deep in meditation that he did not at first notice his visitor, suggested to the chief, a thoughtful person, what manner of man he had before him. He began to converse with his prisoner and brought up a number of questions which had occurred to him in reading the Scriptures. Finally he asked: "How are we to understand that God, the all-knowing, said to Adam: 'Where art thou?'"

"Do you believe," answered the rav, "that the Scriptures are eternal and that every era, every generation and every man is included in them?"

"I believe this," said the other.

"Well then," said the zaddik,[3] "in every era, God calls to every man: 'Where are you in your world? So many years and days of those allotted to you have passed, and how far have you gotten in your world?' God says something like this: 'You have lived forty-six years. How far along are you?' "

When the chief of the gendarmes heard his age mentioned, he pulled himself together, laid his hand on the rav's shoulder, and cried: "Bravo!" But his heart trembled.

What happens in this tale?

At first sight, it reminds us of certain Talmudic stories in which a Roman or some other heathen questions a Jewish sage about a biblical passage with a view to exposing an alleged contradiction in Jewish religious doctrine, and receives a reply which either explains that there is no such contradiction or refutes the questioner's arguments in some other way; sometimes, a personal admonition is added to the actual reply. But we soon perceive an important difference between those Talmudic stories and this hasidic one, though at first the difference appears greater than it actually is. It consists in the fact that in the hasidic story the reply is given on a different plane from that on which the question is asked.

The chief wants to expose an alleged contradiction in Jewish doctrine. The Jews profess to believe in God as the all-knowing, but the Bible makes him ask questions as they are asked by someone who wants to learn something he does not know. God seeks Adam, who has hidden himself. He calls into the garden, asking where he is; it would thus seem that he does not know it, that it is possible to hide from him, and consequently, that he is not all-knowing. Now, instead of explaining the passage and solving the seeming contradiction, the rabbi takes the text merely as a starting-point from where he proceeds to reproach the chief with his past life, his lack of seriousness, his thoughtlessness and irresponsibility. An impersonal question which, however seriously it may be meant in the present instance, is in fact no genuine question but merely a form of controversy, calls forth a personal reply, or rather, a personal admonition in lieu of a reply. It thus seems as if nothing had remained of those Talmudic answers but the admonition which sometimes accompanied them.

But let us examine the story more closely. The chief inquires about a passage from the Biblical story of Adam's sin. The rabbi's answer means, in effect: "You yourself are Adam, you are the man whom God asks: 'Where art thou?' " It would thus seem that the answer gives no explanation of the passage as such. In fact, however, it illuminates both the situation of the biblical Adam and that of every man in every time and in every place. For as soon as

2

the chief hears and understands that the biblical question is addressed to him, he is bound to realize what it means when God asks: "Where art thou?", whether the question be addressed to Adam or to some other man. In so asking, God does not expect to learn something he does not know; what he wants is to produce an effect on man which can only be produced by just such a question, provided that it reaches man's heart — that man allows it to reach his heart.

Adam hides himself to avoid rendering accounts, to escape responsibility for his way of living. Every man hides for this purpose, for every man is Adam and finds himself in Adam's situation. To escape responsibility for his life, he turns existence into a system of hideouts. And in thus hiding again and again "from the face of God," he enmeshes himself more and more deeply in perversity. A new situation thus arises, which becomes more and more questionable with every day, with every new hideout. This situation can be precisely defined as follows: Man cannot escape the eye of God, but in trying to hide from him, he is hiding from himself. True, in him too there is something that seeks him, but he makes it harder and harder for that "something" to find him. This question is designed to awaken man and destroy his system of hideouts; it is to show man to what pass he has come and to awake in him the great will to get out of it.

Everything now depends on whether man faces the question. Of course, every man's heart, like that of the chief in the story, will tremble when he hears it. But his system of hideouts will help him to overcome this emotion. For the Voice does not come in a thunderstorm which threatens man's very existence; it is a "still small voice," and easy to drown. So long as this is done, man's life will not become a *way*. Whatever success and enjoyment he may achieve, whatever power he may attain and whatever deeds he may do, his life will remain way-less, so long as he does not face the Voice. Adam faces the Voice, perceives his enmeshment, and avows: "I hid myself;" this is the beginning of man's way. The decisive heart-searching is the beginning of the way in man's life; it is, again and again, the beginning of a human way. But heart-searching is decisive only if it leads to the way. For there is a sterile kind of heart-searching, which leads to nothing but self-torture, despair and still deeper enmeshment. When the Rabbi of Ger,[4] in expounding the Scriptures, came to the words which Jacob addresses to his servants: "When Esau my brother meets thee, and asks thee, saying, Whose art thou? and whither goest thou? and whose are these before thee?," he would say to his disciples: "Mark well how similar Esau's questions are to the saying of our sages: 'Consider three things. Know whence you came, whither you are going, and to whom you will have to render accounts.' Be very careful, for great caution should be exercised by him who considers these three things: lest Esau ask in him. For Esau, too, may ask these questions and bring man into a state of gloom."

There is a demonic question, a spurious question, which apes God's question, the question of Truth. Its characteristic is that it does not stop at: "Where art thou?" but continues: "From where you have got to, there is no way out." This is the wrong kind of heart-searching, which does not prompt man to turn, and put him on the way, but, by representing turning as hopeless, drives him to a point where it appears to have become entirely impossible and man can go on living only by demonic pride, the pride of perversity.

II. The Particular Way

Rabbi Baer of Radoshitz once said to his teacher, the "Seer" of Lublin: "Show me one general way to the service of God."

The zaddik replied: "It is impossible to tell men what way they should take. For one way to serve God is through learning, another through prayer, another through fasting, and still another through eating. Everyone should carefully observe what way his heart draws him to, and then choose this way with all his strength."

In the first place, this story tells us something about our relationship to such genuine service as was performed by others before us. We are to revere it and learn from it, but we are not to imitate it. The great and holy deeds done by others are examples for us, since they show, in a concrete manner, what greatness and holiness is, but they are not models which we should copy. However small our achievements may be in comparison with those of our forefathers, they have their real value in that we bring them about in our own way and by our own efforts.

The maggid[5] of Zlotchov[6] was asked by a hasid: "We are told: 'Everyone in Israel is on duty bound to say: When will my work approach the works of my fathers, Abraham, Issac and Jacob?' How are we to understand this? How could we ever venture to think that we could do what our fathers did?"

The rabbi expounded: "Just as our fathers founded new ways of serving, each a new service according to his character: one the service of love, the other that of stern justice, the third that of beauty, so each one of us in his own way shall devise something new in the light of teachings and of service, and do what has not yet been done."

Every person born into this world represents something new, something that never existed before, something original and unique. "It is the duty of every person in Israel to know and consider that he is unique in the world in his particular character and that there has never been anyone like him in the world, for if there had been someone like him, there would have been no need for him to be in the world. Every single man is a new thing in the world, and is called upon to fulfill his particularity in this world. For verily: that this is not done, is the reason why the coming of the Messiah is delayed." Every man's foremost task is the actualization of his unique, unprecedented and never-recurring potentialities, and not the repetition of something that another, and be it even the greatest, has already achieved.

The wise Rabbi Bunam once said in old age, when he had already grown blind: "I should not like to change places with our father Abraham! What good would it do God if Abraham became like a blind Bunam, and blind Bunam became like Abraham? Rather than have this happen, I think I shall try to become a little more like myself."

The same idea was expressed with even greater pregnancy by Rabbi Zusya when he said, a short while before his death: "In the world to come I shall not be asked: 'Why were you not Moses?' I shall be asked: 'Why were you not Zusya?' "

We are here confronted with a doctrine which is based on the fact that men are essentially unlike one another, and which therefore does not aim at making them alike. All men have access to God, but each man has a different access. Mankind's great chance lies precisely in the unlikeness of men, in the unlikeness of their qualities and inclinations. God's all-inclusiveness manifests itself in the infinite multiplicity of the ways that lead to him, each of which is open to one man. When some disciples of a deceased zaddik came to the "Seer" of Lublin and expressed surprise at the fact that his customs were different from those of their late master, the "Seer" exclaimed: "What sort of God would that be who has only one way in which he can be served!" But by the fact that each man, starting from his particular place and in a manner determined by his particular nature, is able to reach God, God can be reached by mankind as such, through its multiple advance by all those different ways.

God does not say: "This way leads to me and that does not," but he says: "Whatever you do may be a way to me, provided you do it in such a manner that it leads you to me." But what it is that can and shall be done by just this person and no other, can be revealed to him only in himself. In this manner, as I said before it would only be misleading to study the achievements of another and endeavour to equal him; for in so doing, a man would miss precisely what he and he alone is called upon to do. The Baal-Shem[7] said: "Every man should behave according to his 'rung.' If he does not, if he seizes the 'rung' of a fellow-man and abandons his own, he will acutalize neither the one nor the other." Thus, the way by which a man can reach God is revealed to him only through the knowledge of his own being, the knowledge of his essential quality and inclination. "Everyone has in him something precious that is in no one else." But this precious something in a man is revealed to him only if he truly perceives his strongest feelings, his central wish, that in him which stirs his inmost being.

Of course, in many cases, a man knows this his strongest feeling only in the shape of a particular passion, of the "Evil Urge" which seeks to lead him astray. Naturally, a man's most powerful desire, in seeking satisfaction, rushes in the first instance at objects which lie across his path. It is necessary, therefore, that the power of even this feeling, of even this impulse, be diverted from the casual to the essential, and from the relative to the absolute. Thus a man finds his way.

A zaddik once said: "At the end of Ecclesiastes we read: 'At the end of the matter, the whole is heard: Fear God.' Whatever matter you follow to its end, there, at the end, you will hear one thing: 'Fear God,' and this one thing is the whole. There is no thing in the world which does not point a way to the fear of God and to the service of God. Everything is commandment." By no means, however, can it be our true task in the world into which we have been set, to turn away from the things and beings that we meet on our way and that attract our hearts; our task is precisely to get in touch, by hallowing our relationship with them, with what manifests itself in them as beauty, pleasure, enjoyment. Hasidism teaches that rejoicing in the world, if we hallow it with our whole being, leads to rejoicing in God.

One point in the tale of the "Seer" seems to contradict this, namely, that among the examples of "ways" we find not only eating but also fasting. But if we consider this in the general context of hasidic teaching, it appears that though detachment from nature, abstinence from natural life, may, in the cases of some men mean the necessary starting-point of their "way" or, perhaps, a necessary act of self-isolation at certain crucial moments of existence, it may never mean the whole way. Some men must begin fasting, and begin by it again and again, because it is peculiar to them that only by asceticism can they achieve liberation from their enslavement to the world, deepest heart-searching and ultimate communion with the Absolute. But never should asceticism gain mastery over a man's life. A man may only detach himself from nature in order to revert to it again and, in hallowed contact with it, find his way to God.

The biblical passage which says of Abraham and the three visiting angels: "And he stood over them under the tree and they did eat" is interpreted by Rabbi Zusya to the effect that man stands above the angels, because he knows something unknown to them, namely, that eating may be hallowed by the eater's intention. Through Abraham the angels, who were unaccustomed to eating, participated in the intention by which he used to dedicate it to God. Any natural act, if hallowed, leads to God, and nature needs man for what no angel can perform on it, namely, its hallowing.

Footnotes:

1. Rabbi.
2. i.e., adversaries (of Hasidism).
3. i.e., proved true; so the leaders of the Hasidic communities are called.
4. i.e., Góra Kalwarya near Warsaw.
5. i.e., preacher.
6. Town in Eastern Galicia.
7. i.e., Master of the Name (of God). So the founder of Hasidism, Rabbi Israel ben Eliezer (1700-1760), was surnamed.

The Sigh

Abraham Joshua Heschel

Abraham Joshua Heschel (1907-1972) is, like Buber, a Jewish theologian with a wide Christian readership. Deported from Germany by the Nazis in 1938, he went first to the Institute for Jewish Learning in London, and then emigrated to the United States where he taught at Hebrew Union College in Cincinnati. In 1945 he moved to New York and joined the faculty of the Jewish Theological Seminary of America, where he taught until his death. The following moving meditation on prayer is typical of Heschel's writing, which is at once lyrical and profoundly realistic.

About a hundred years ago, Rabbi Isaac Meir Alter of Ger pondered over the question of what a certain shoemaker of his acquaintance should do about his morning prayer. His customers were poor men who owned only one pair of shoes. The shoemaker used to pick up their shoes at a late evening hour, work on them all night and part of the morning, in order to deliver them before their owners had to go to work. When should the shoemaker say his morning prayer? Should he pray quickly the first thing in the morning, and then go back to work? Or should he let the appointed hour of prayer go by and, every once in a while, raising his hammer from the shoes, utter a sigh: "Woe unto me, I haven't prayed yet!"? Perhaps that sigh is worth more than the prayer itself.

We, too, face this dilemma of wholehearted regret or perfunctory fulfillment. Many of us regretfully refrain from habitual prayer, waiting for an urge that is complete, sudden, and unexampled. But the unexampled is scarce, and perpetual refraining can easily grow into a habit. We may even come to forget what to regret, what to miss.

Abraham Joshua Heschel

The Ability to Answer

We do not refuse to pray. We merely feel that our tongues are tied, our minds inert, our inner vision dim, when we are about to enter the door that leads to prayer. We do not refuse to pray; we abstain from it. We ring the hollow bell of selfishness rather than absorb the stillness that surrounds the world, hovering over all the restlessness and fear of life — the secret stillness that precedes our birth and succeeds our death. Futile self-indulgence brings us out of tune with the gentle song of nature's waiting, of mankind's striving for salvation. Is not listening to the pulse of wonder worth silence and abstinence from self-assertion? Why do we not set apart an hour of living for devotion to God by surrendering to stillness? We dwell on the edge of mystery and ignore it, wasting our souls, risking our stake in God. We constantly pour our inner light away from Him, setting up the thick screen of self between Him and us, adding more shadows to the darkness that already hovers between Him and our wayward reason. Accepting surmises as dogmas, and prejudices as solutions, we ridicule the evidence of life for what is more than life. Our mind has ceased to be sensitive to the wonder. Deprived of the power of devotion to what is more important than our individual fate, steeped in passionate anxiety to survive, we lose sight of what fate is, of what living is. Rushing through the ecstasies of ambition, we only awake when plunged into dread or grief. In darkness, then, we grope for solace, for meaning, for prayer.

But there is a wider voluntary entrance to prayer than sorrow and despair — the opening of our thoughts to God. We cannot make Him visible to us, but we can make ourselves visible to Him. So we open our thoughts to Him — feeble our tongues, but sensitive our hearts. We see more than we can say. The trees stand like guards of the Everlasting; the flowers like signposts of His goodness — only *we* have failed to be testimonies to His presence, tokens of His trust. How could we have lived in the shadow of greatness and defied it?

Mindfulness of God rises slowly, a thought at a time. Suddenly we are there. Or is He here, at the margin of our soul? When we begin to feel a qualm of diffidence lest we hurt what is holy, lest we break what is whole, then we discover that He is not austere. He answers with love our trembling awe. Repentant of forgetting Him even for a while, we become sharers of gentle joy; we would like to dedicate ourselves forever to the unfoldment of His final order.

To pray is to take notice of the wonder, to regain a sense of the

9

mystery that animates all beings, the divine margin in all attainments. Prayer is *our* humble *answer* to the inconceivable surprise of living. It is all we can offer in return for the mystery by which we live. Who is worthy to be present at the constant unfolding of time? Amidst the meditation of mountains, the humility of flowers — wiser than all alphabets — clouds that die constantly for the sake of His glory, *we* are hating, hunting, hurting. Suddenly we feel ashamed of our clashes and complaints in the face of the tacit glory in nature. It is so embarrassing to live! How strange we are in the world, and how presumptuous our doings! Only one response can maintain us: gratefulness for witnessing the wonder, for the gift of our unearned right to serve, to adore, and to fulfill. It is gratefulness which makes the soul great.

However, we often lack the strength to be grateful, the courage to answer, the ability to pray. To escape from the mean and penurious, from calculating and scheming, is at times the parching desire of man. Tired of discord, he longs to escape from his own mind — and for the peace of prayer. How good it is to wrap oneself in prayer, spinning a deep softness of gratitude to God around all thoughts, enveloping oneself in the silken veil of song! But how can man draw song out of his heart if his consciousness is a woeful turmoil of fear and ambition? He has nothing to offer but disgust, and the weariness of wasting the soul. Accustomed to winding strands of thoughts, to twisting phrases in order to be successful, he is incapable of finding simple, straight words. His language abounds in traps and decoys, in shams and tricks, in gibes and sneers. In the teeth of such powerful distractions, he has to focus all the powers of his mind on one concern. In the midst of universal agitation, how can there be tranquillity?

Trembling in the realization that we are a blend of modesty and insolence, of self-denial and bias, we beseech God for rescue, for help in the control of our thoughts, words, and deeds. We lay all our forces before Him. Prayer is arrival at the border. The dominion is Thine. Take away from me all that may not enter Thy realm.

The Essence of Spiritual Living

As a tree torn from the soil, as a river separated from its source, the human soul wanes when detached from what is greater than itself. Without the holy, the good turns chaotic; without the good, beauty becomes accidental. It is the pattern of the impeccable which makes the average possible. It is the attachment to what is spiritually superior: loyalty to a sacred person or idea, devotion to a noble friend or teacher, love for a people or for mankind, which holds our inner life together. But any ideal, human, social, or artistic, if it forms a roof over all of life, shuts us off from the light. Even the palm of one hand may bar the light of the entire sun. Indeed, we must be open to the remote in order to perceive the near. Unless we aspire to the utmost, we shrink to inferiority.

Prayer is our attachment to the utmost. Without God in sight, we are like the scattered rungs of a broken ladder. To pray is to become a ladder on which thoughts mount to God to join the movement toward Him which surges unnoticed throughout the entire universe. We do not step out of the world when we pray; we merely see the world in a different setting. The self is not the hub, but the spoke of the revolving wheel. In prayer we shift the center of living from self-consciousness to self-surrender. God is the center toward which all forces tend. He is the source, and we are the flowing of His force, the ebb and flow of His tides.

Prayer takes the mind out of the narrowness of self-interest, and enables us to see the world in the mirror of the holy. For when we betake ourselves to the extreme opposite of the ego, we can behold a situation from the aspect of God. Prayer is a way to master what is inferior in us, to discern between the signal and the trivial, between the vital and the futile, by taking counsel with what we know about the will of God, by seeing our fate in proportion to God. Prayer clarifies our hope and intentions. It helps us to discover our true aspirations, the pangs we ignore, the longings we forget. It is an act of self-purification, a quarantine for the soul. It gives us the opportunity to be honest, to say what we believe, and to stand for what we say. For the accord of assertion and conviction, of thought and conscience, is the basis of all prayer.

Prayer teaches us what to aspire to. So often we do not know what to cling to. Prayer implants in us the ideals we ought to cherish. Redemption, purity of mind and tongue, or willingness to help, may hover as ideas before our mind, but the idea becomes a concern, something to long for, a goal to be reached, when we pray: "Guard my tongue from evil and my lips from speaking guile; and in the face of those who curse me, let my soul be silent."[1]

Prayer is the essence of spiritual living. Its spell is present in every spiritual experience. Its drive enables us to delve into what is what beneath our beliefs and desires, and to emerge with a renewed taste for the infinite simplicity of the good. On the globe of the microcosm the flow of prayer is like the Gulf Stream, imparting warmth to all that is cold, melting all that is hard in our life. For even loyalties may freeze to indifference if detached from the stream which carries the strength to be loyal. How often does justice lapse into cruelty, and righteousness into hypocrisy. Prayer revives and keeps alive the rare greatness of some past experience in which things glowed with meaning and blessing. It remains important, even when we ignore it for a while, like a candlestick set aside for the day. Night will come, and we shall again gather round its tiny flame. Our affection for the trifles of living will be mixed with longing for the comfort of all men.

However, prayer is no panacea, no subsititute for action. It is, rather, like a beam thrown from a flashlight before us into the darkness. It is in this light that we who grope, stumble and climb, discover where we stand, what surrounds us, and the course which we should choose. Prayer makes visible the right, and reveals what is hampering and false. In its radiance, we behold the worth of our efforts, the range of our hopes, and the meaning of our deeds. Envy and fear, despair and resentment, anguish and grief, which lie heavily upon the heart, are dispelled like shadows by its light.

Sometimes prayer is more than a light before us; it is a light within us. Those who have once been resplendent with this light find little meaning in speculations about the efficacy of prayer. A story is told about a Rabbi who once entered heaven in a dream. He was permitted to approach the temple of Paradise where the great sages of the Talmud, the Tannaim, were spending their eternal lives. He saw that they were just sitting around tables studying the Talmud. The disappointed Rabbi wondered, "Is this all there is to Paradise?" But suddenly he heard a voice, "You are mistaken. The Tannaim are not in Paradise. Paradise is in the Tannaim."

Man's Ultimate Aspiration

In those souls in which prayer is a rare flower, enchanting, surprising, it seems to come to pass by the lucky chance of misfortune, as an inevitable or adventitious by-product of affliction. But suffering is not the source of prayer. A motive does not bring about an act as a cause produces an effect; it merely stimulates the potential into becoming an actuality. Peril or want may clear the ground for its growth, stubbing up the weeds of self-assurance, ridding the heart of the hard and obdurate, but it can never raise prayer.

To a farmer about to prepare a seedbed, the prerequisite for his undertaking is not the accidental need of a crop. His need of food does not endow him with skill in cultivating the earth; it merely affords the stimulus and purpose for his undertaking. It is his knowledge, his possession of the idea of tillage, which enables him to raise crops. The same principle applies to prayer. The natural loyalty of living, fertilized by faith saved through a lifetime, is the soil on which prayer can grow. Laden with secret fertility and patient discreetness concerning things to be and things forever unknown, the soil of the soul nourishes and holds the roots of prayer. But the soil by itself does not produce crops. There must also be the idea of prayer to make the soul yield its amazing fruit.

The idea of prayer is based upon the assumption of man's ability to accost God, to lay our hopes, sorrows and wishes before Him. But this assumption is not an awareness of a particular ability with which we are endowed. We do not feel that we possess a magic power of speaking to the Infinite; we merely witness the wonder of prayer, the wonder of man addressing himself to the Eternal. Contact with Him is not our achievement. It is a gift, coming down to us from on high like a meteor. rather than rising up like a rocket. Before the words of prayer come to the lips, the mind must believe in God's willingness to draw near to us, and in our ability to clear the path for His approach. Such belief is the idea that leads us toward prayer.

Prayer is not a soliloquy. But is it a dialogue with God?[2] Does man address Him as person to person? It is incorrect to describe prayer by analogy with human conversation; we do not communicate with God. We only make ourselves communicable to Him. Prayer is an emanation of what is most precious in us toward Him, the outpouring of the heart before Him. It is not a relationship between person and person, between subject and subject, but an endeavor to become the object of His thought.

Prayer is like the light from a burning glass in which all the rays that emanate from the soul are gathered to a focus. There are hours when we are resplendent with the glowing awareness of our share in His secret interest on earth. We pray. We are carried forward to Him who is coming close to us. We endeavor to divine His will, not merely His command. Prayer is an answer to God: "Here am I. And this is the record of my days. Look into my heart, into my hopes and my regrets." We depart in shame and joy. Yet prayer never ends, for faith endows us with a bold craving that He draw near to us and approach us as a father — not only as a ruler; not only through our walking in His ways, but through His entering into our ways. The purpose of prayer is to be brought to His attention, to be listened to, to be understood by Him, not to know Him, but to *be known* to Him. To pray is to behold life not only as a result of His power, but as a concern of His will, or to strive to make our life a divine concern. For the ultimate aspiration of man is not to be a master, but an object of His knowledge. To live "in the light of His countenance," to become a thought of God — this is the true career of man.

But are we worthy of being known, of entering into His mercy, of being a matter of concern to Him? It seems as if the meaning of prayer lies in man's aspiration to be thought of by God as one who is thinking of Him. Man waxes in God when serving the sacred, and wanes when he betrays his task. Man lives in His mind when He abides in man's life.

There is no human misery more strongly felt than the state of being forsaken by God. Nothing is so terrible as rejection by Him. It is a horror to live deserted by God, and effaced from His mind. The fear of being forgotten even for an instant is a powerful spur to a pious man to bring himself to the attention of God, to keep his life *worth* being known to Him. He prefers to be smitten by His punishment rather than to be left alone. In all his prayers he begs, explicitly or implicitly, "Do not forsake me, O Lord."

The man who betrays Him day after day, drunk with vanity, resentment, or reckless ambition, lives in a ghostly mist of misgivings. Having ruined love with greed, he is still wondering about the lack of tenderness in his own life. His soul contains a hiding-place for an escaping conscience. He has torn his ties to God into shreds of shrieking dread, and his mind remains dull and callous. Spoiler of his own lot, he walks the earth a skeleton of a soul, raving about missed delight.

God is not alone when discarded by man. But man is alone. To avoid prayer constantly is to force a gap between man and God which can widen into an abyss. But sometimes, awakening on the edge of despair to weep, and arising from forgetfulness, we feel how yearning moves in softly to become the lord of a restless breast, and we pass over the gap with the lightness of a dream.

Footnotes:

1. From the daily liturgy.
2. Prayer is defined as a dialogue with God by Clement of Alexandria. See Max Pohlenz, *Die Stoa*, Geschichte einer geistigen Bewegung, Goettingen, 1948, Vol. I, p. 423.

Spiritual Life

Evelyn Underhill

Evelyn Underhill (1875-1941) was the author of many works of theology and poetry; she is best known for Mysticism, *which was originally published in 1911 and is still widely read. Although she remained devoutly Anglican all her life, she was open to the spiritual and liturgical influences of other Christian traditions, particularly Orthodoxy and Roman Catholicism.*

"Spiritual Life" is a very elastic phrase; which can either be made to mean the most hazy religiosity and most objectionable forms of uplift, or be limited to the most exclusive types of contemplation. Yet surely we should not mean by it any of these things, but something which for most of us is much more actual, more concrete; indeed, an essential constituent of all human life worthy of the name. I am not proposing to talk about mystics, or any one who has rare and peculiar religious experience: but simply about ourselves, normal people living the natural social and intellectual life of our time. If we know much about ourselves, I think we must agree that there is something in us which, in spite of all the efforts of a materialistic psychology, is not accounted for either by the requirements of natural life or those of social life; and which cannot altogether be brought within the boundaries of the intellectual and rational life. Though as it develops this "something" will penetrate and deeply affect all these levels of our existence, we recognize that it is distinct from them. It is an element which is perhaps usually dormant; yet is sometimes able to give us strange joys, and sometimes strange discomforts. It points beyond our visible environment to something else; to a Reality which transcends the time-series, and yet to which we, because of the existence of this quality in us, are somehow akin.

By talking of "spirit" or "spiritual life" — terms more allusive than exact — we do not make these facts less mysterious. But we do make it possible to think about them, and consider what they must involve for our view of the nature of Reality; what light they cast on the nature of man; and finally how this quality which we call "spiritual life" calls us, as spirits, to act. In other words, we are brought up against the three primary data of religion: God, the soul, and the relation between God and the soul. Those three points, I think, cover the main aspects of man's life as spirit. They become, as he grows in spiritual awareness and responsiveness, more and more actual to him, and more and more fully incorporated in his experience. And they are all three represented in the life of prayer; which, taken in the widest sense, is the peculiar spiritual activity of man. By prayer, of course, I do not merely mean primitive prayer — the clamour of the childish creature for help, relief or gifts from beyond — though this survives in us, as all our primitive and instinctive life still survives. I mean the developed prayer of the soul which has taken its Godward life, its link with the Eternal, seriously; has knocked and had a door opened on to a fresh range of experience. Such prayer as that is just as much a human fact as great achievement in music or poetry; and must be taken into account in estimating the possibilities of human life.

We begin then with this fact of something in us which points beyond physical life, however complete that physical life may be, and suggests — perhaps in most of us, very faintly and occasionally, but in some with a decisive authority — that somehow we are borderland creatures. As human beings, we stand between an order of things which we know very well, to which most of us are more or less adapted, and in which we can easily immerse ourselves; and another order, of which we do not know much, but which, if we respond to it, can gradually become the most important factor in our lives. We might sum this up by saying that there is in us a fringe-region where human personality ceases to be merely natural, and takes up characteristics from another order; yet without losing concrete hold upon what we call natural life. It is in this fringe-region of our being that religion is born. It points to the fact that we need to be met and completed by an order of being, a Reality, that lies beyond us. We are in the making; and such significance as we have is the significance of a still unfinished thing.

Of course, in the pitter-patter of temporal existence it is very easy to lose all sense of this otherness and incompleteness of life; this mysterious quality in human nature. Attention, will and intelligence have all been trained in response to the physical; and turn most easily that way. We live too in a time of immense corporate self-consciousness. Modern literature, with its perpetual preoccupation with the details of our emotional and sexual relationships, reflects this. Universals, and our relation to universals, are neglected. Yet without some recognition of our relation to Reality, we are only half-human; and if we are alert, we cannot entirely miss all conciousness of the presence and pressure of that Reality, that eternal order, however we may represent it to ourselves. The strange little golden intimations of beauty and holiness that flash up through life, however they come, do present a fundamental problem to us. Are these intimations of Reality in its most precious aspect, the faint beginnings of an experience, a development of life, towards which we can move; or are they mere will-o'-the-wisps? Shall we trust them and give them priority, or regard them with the curiosity that borders on contempt?

In other words, is reality spiritual? Is the only concrete reality God, as the mystics have always declared? And is that richly real and living God present to and pressing upon His whole creation; or is this merely a pious idea? Are man's small spiritual experiences testimonies to a vast truth, which in its wholeness lies far beyond us, or not? We have to choose between these alternatives; and the choice will settle the character of our religion and philosophy, and will also colour the whole texture of existence, the way we do our daily jobs.

We assume that the first alternative is the true one; that men are created spirits in the making, and can experience a communion with that Living God, Spirit of all spirits, who is the Reality of the universe. What we call our religious experiences, are genuine if fragmentary glimpses of this Divine Reality. That belief, of course, lies at the very heart of real Christian theism. In thinking about it, we are not moving off to some peculiar or specialized mystical religion; we are exploring the treasures of our common faith. And the first point that comes out of it for us, I think, is the distinctness and independence of God and of Eternal Life: as realities so wholly other than the natural order and the natural creature, that they must be given us from beyond ourselves. A great deal of modern Christianity, especially that type which is anxious to come to terms with theories of emergent evolution and other forms of immanentism, seems to me to be poisoned by a kind of spiritual self-sufficiency; which tends to blur this fundamental and humbling distinction between the creature and God, and between the natural and spiritual life. It perpetually suggests that all we have to do is to grow, develop, unpack our own spiritual suit-cases; that nothing need be given us or done to us from beyond.

Were the fullest possible development of his natural resources the real end of the being of man, this might be true enough. But all the giants of the spiritual life are penetrated through and through be the conviction that this is not the goal of human existence: that something must be given, or done to them, from the eternal world over-against us, without which man can never be complete. They feel, however variously they express it, that for us in our strange borderland situation there must be two orders, two levels of reality, two mingled lives, to both of which we are required to re-spond — the natural and the spiritual, nature and grace, life towards man and life towards God — and that the life of spirit of which we are capable must come to us, before we can go to it. It is surely the true instinct of religion which fills the liturgy with references to something which must be given or poured out on us. "Pour down on us the continual dew of Thy blessing" — "Pour into our hearts such love towards Thee" — "Without Thee we are not able to please Thee." All summed up in the wonderful prayer of St. Augustine: "Give what Thou dost demand; and then, demand what Thou wilt."

So I suppose, from the human point of view, a spiritual life is a life which is controlled by a gradually developing sense of the Eternal, of God and His transcendent reality; an increasing capacity for Him, so that our relation to God becomes the chief thing about us, exceeding and also conditioning our relationship with each other. So here the first and second points which we were to con-sider — what we mean by a spiritual life, and what a spiritual life involves for us — seem to melt into one other. Indeed, it is almost impossible to consider them separately. For, what it means for us is surely this: that we are meant, beyond the physical, to contribute to, indeed collaborate in, God's spiritual creation; to be the willing and vigorous tools and channels of His action in Time. That is the spiritual life of man at its fullest development, the life of all great personalities; saints, artists, explorers, servants of science. It is a life infinite in its variety of expression, but marked by a certain deep eternal quality, a disinterested zest for perfection, in all its temporal acts.

When we come to make the personal application of these ideas, this view of the relation of our fluid, half-made personalities to God, and ask how, as individuals, we are called to act — and that is the third of the questions with which we started — we see that just in so far as this view of human life is realistic, it lays on each of us a great and a distinct obligation. Though the life of the Spirit comes from God, the ocean of our being, *we* have to do something about it. Utter dependence on God must be balanced by courageous initiative. Each of us has a double relationship, and is required to develop a double correspondence. First with the Divine Creative Spirit who penetrates and supports our spirits; and secondly with the universe of souls, which is enlaced with us in one vast web of being — whether our immediate neighbours of the Christian family who form with us part of the Mystical Body of Christ, or the more widespread corporation of all the children of God, of which this perhaps forms the nucleus.

For those who see life thus, sustained and fed by a present God, and who can say with St. Augustine "I should not exist wert not Thou already with me," the idea of mere self-determination, self-expression as an end in itself, becomes ridiculous. Further than this, the notion of souls, persons, as separate ring-fenced units, is also seen to be impossible. In many ways that are perceptible, and many others so subtle as to be imperceptible, we penetrate and affect one another. The mysterious thing called influence points to our far-reaching power and responsibility, and the plastic character of the human self. Because of this plasticity, this inter-penetration of spirits; those who have developed their capacity for God, have learnt, as St. John of the Cross says, how to direct their wills vigorously towards Him, can and do become channels along which His life and power can secretly but genuinely transform some bit of life. Devotion by itself has little value, may even by itself be a form of self-indulgence, unless it issues in some costly and self-giving action of this kind. The spiritual life of any individual, therefore, has to be extended both vertically to God and horizontally to other souls; and the more it grows in both directions, the less merely individual and therefore the more truly personal it will be. It is, in the truest sense, in humanity that we grow by this incorporation of the spiritual and temporal, the deeps and the surface of life; getting more not less rich, various and supple in our living out of existence. Seen from the spiritual angle, Christians selves are simply parts of that vast organism the Church Invisible, which is called upon to incarnate the Divine Life in history, and bring eternity into time. Each one of us has his own place in this scheme, and each is required to fulfil a particular bit of that plan by which the human world is being slowly lifted God-ward, and the Kingdom of God is brought in. This double action — interior and ever-deepening communion with God, and because of it ever-widening outgoing towards the world as tools and channels of God, the balanced life of faith and works, surrender and activity — must always involve a certain tension between the two movements. Nor, as St. Paul saw, should we expect the double movement to be produced quite perfectly in any one individual: not even in the saints. The body has many members, some of them a very funny shape, but each with their own job. The man of prayer and the man of action balance and complete one another. Every genuine vocation must play its part in this transformation in God of the whole complex life of man.

Men are the only created beings of which we have knowledge, who are aware of this call, this need of putting themselves in one way or another at the disposal of Creative Spirit; and this characteristic, even though it be only occasionally developed to the full in human nature, assures us that there is in that nature a certain kinship with God. So every human soul without exception, because of this its mysterious affinity with God, and yet its imperfect status, its unlikeness from God, is called to undertake a growth and a transformation; which shall make of it a channel of the Divine energy and will. Such a statement as this, of course, is not to be narrowed down and limited to that which we call the "religious" life. On the contrary it affirms the religious character of all full life. For it means a kind of self-oblivious faithfulness in response to all the various demands of circumstance, the carrying through of everything to which one sets one's hand, which is rooted in a deep — though not necessarily emotional — loyalty to the interests of God. That conception expands our idea of the religious life far beyond the devotional life; till there is room in it for all the multiple activities of man in so far as they are prosecuted in, for, and with the Fact of all facts, God-Reality. I need not point out that for Christians the Incarnation — the entrance of God into History — and its extension in the Church bring together these two movements in the soul and in the human complex; and start a vast process, to which every awakened soul which rises above self-interest has some contribution to make. As we become spiritually sensitive, and more alert in our response to experience, I think we sometimes get a glimpse of that deep creative action by which we are being brought into this new order of being, more and more transformed into the agents of spirit; able to play our part in the great human undertaking of bringing the whole world nearer to the intention of God. We then perceive the friction of circumstance, the hard and soft of life, personal contacts and opportunities, love and pain and dreariness, to be penetrated and used by a Living Influence, which is making by this means both changes and positive additions to our human nature; softening, deepening, enriching and moulding the raw material of temperament into something nearer the artist's design.

Next, let us look for a moment at Prayer, as the special reflection and expression of this relation of God and soul of which we have been thinking. Prayer is, if not the guarantee, at least a mighty witness to the reality of the spiritual life. If we were merely clever animals, had no kinship with God, we could not pray: no communion between Him and us would be possible. Prayer, in its three great forms of Worship, Communion and Intercession, is after all a purely spiritual activity; an acknowledgement of the supreme reality and power of the spiritual life in man. As St. Thomas says, it is a "marvellous intercourse between Infinite and finite, God and the soul."

If the first term of the spiritual life is recognition in some way or other of the splendour and reality of God, the first mood of prayer — the ground from which all the rest must grow — is certainly worship, awe, adoration; delight in that holy reality for its own sake. This truth has lately returned to the foreground of religious thought; and there is little need to insist on it afresh. Religion, as von Hügel loved to say, *is* adoration; man's humble acknowledgement of the Transcendent, the Fact of God — the awestruck realism of the seraphs in Isaiah's vision — the meek and loving sense of mystery which enlarges the soul's horizon and and puts us in our place. Prayer, which is so much more a state and condition of soul than a distinct act, begins there; in the lifting of the eyes of the little creature to the Living God, or perhaps to the symbol through which the Living God reveals Himself to the soul.

It is mainly because we are unaccustomed to a spiritual outlook which is centred on the infinite mystery of God and not merely on ourselves and our own need and desires, that we so easily become confused by the changes and chances of experience. And for modern men, confronted as we all are by a swiftly changing physical and mental universe, sweeping away as it must many old symbolic constructions, but giving in their place a fresh and humbling sense of the height and depth and breadth of Creation and our own small place in it, it is surely imperative to establish and feed this adoring sense of the unchanging Reality of God. It is easy, so long as the emphasis lies on us and our immediate interests, to be baffled and depressed by a sense of our own futility. Our whole life may seem to be penned down to attending to the horrid little tea-shop in the valley; yet this and every other vocation is ennobled, if we find time each day to lift our eyes to the everlasting snows. I think we might make far greater efforts than we do, to get this adoring remembrance of the Reality of God, who alone gives our work significance, woven into our everyday lives. There is no more certain method of evicting pettiness, self-occupation and unrest; those deadly enemies of the spiritual self.

It is within this penetrating sense of God Present yet Transcendent, which braces and humbles us both at once, that the second stage of prayer — a personal self-giving that culminates in a personal communion — emerges and grows. Here we have the personal response and relationship of the self to that God who has evoked our worship. Adoration, as it more deeply possesses us, inevitably leads on to self-offering: for every advance in prayer is really an advance in love. "I ask not for thy gifts but for thyself" says the Divine Voice to Thomas à Kempis. There is something in all of us which knows that to be true. True, because of the fact of human freedom; because human beings have the awful power of saying Yes or No to God and His purposes, linking up our separate actions with the great divine action, or pursuing a self-centred or earth-centred course. This is the heart of practical religion, and can be tested on the common stuff of our daily lives. It is this face of freedom which makes Sacrifice, with its elements of personal cost and confident approach, and its completion in communion, the most perfect symbol of the soul's intimate and personal approach to God. If worship is the lifting up towards the Infinite of the eyes of faith, self-offering is the prayer of hope: the small and fugitive creature giving itself, its thoughts, deeds, desires in entire confidence to the mysterious purposes of Eternal Life. It is summed up in the great prayer of St. Ignatius: "Take Lord, and receive!"

But as the realistic sense of God in Himself which is the basis of adoration leads on to a realistic personal relationship with Him in self-offering and communion, there develops that full and massive type of prayer in which spiritual power is developed, and human creatures become fellow workers with the Spirit, tools and channels through which God's creative work is done. That is the life of Charity: the life of friendship with God, for which we were made. Growth in spiritual personality means growth in charity. And charity — energetic love of God, and of all men in God — operating in the world of prayer, is the live wire along which the Power of God, indwelling our finite spirits, can and does act on other souls and other things; rescuing, healing, giving support and light. That, of course, is real intercession; which is gravely misunderstood by us, if we think of it mainly in terms of asking God to grant particular needs and desires. Such secret intercessory prayer ought to penetrate and accompany all our active work, if it is really to be turned to the purposes of God. It is the supreme expression of the spiritual life on earth: moving from God to man, through us, because we have ceased to be self-centred units, but are woven into the great fabric of praying souls, the "mystical body" through which the work of Christ on earth goes on being done. We talk about prayer thus by means of symbols; but as a matter of fact we cannot really rationalize it without impoverishing it. It leads us into the world of mystery where the Creative Spirit operates; in ways beyond and above all we can conceive, yet along paths which touch and can transform at every point our humble daily lives and activities. Thus prayer, as the heart of man's spiritual life — his Godward response and striving — is seen to be something which far exceeds devotional exercises; and is and must be present in all disinterested striving for perfection, for Goodness, for Truth and Beauty, or for the betterment of the children of God. For it means the increasing dedication and possession of all our faculties by Him; the whole drive of our active will subdued to His design, penetrated by His Life and used for His ends.

And last, coming down to ourselves, how does all this work out in the ordinary Christian life? It works out, I think, as a gradual growth in the soul's adherence to God and co-operation with God, achieved by three chief means: 1. Discipline, mental, moral, and devotional. 2. Symbolic and sacramental acts. 3. Ever-renewed and ever more perfect dedication of the will; death to self. This point, of course, is incomparably the most important. The others have their chief meaning in the fact that they contribute to and support it.

Discipline. This includes the gradual training of our faculties to attend to God, by the regular practice of meditation and recollected vocal prayer. Also such moral drill as shall conduce to the conquest of the instinctive nature; the triumph of what traditional asceticism calls the "superior faculties of the soul," or, in plain English, getting ourselves thoroughly in hand. At least, in the experience of most souls, this will involve a certain moderate amount of real asceticism, a painful effort to mortify faults of character, especially those which are ramifications of self-love, and a humble submission to elementary education in devotional routine. Under this head we get an ordered rule of life, voluntary self-denials, and a careful detachment of the emotions from all overwhelming attractions which compete with God. Acceptance of the general methods and regulations of the Church also comes in here, as the first stage in that very essential process, the socializing and incorporation of the individual life of prayer; that it may find its place, and make its contribution to the total life of the Mystical Body of Christ. None of this is actual prayer; but all of it, in various degrees, must enter into the preparation of the self for prayer.

Next, *Symbolic Acts.* Even if we can dare to say that there is such a thing as an absolute, and purely spiritual communication of God with the soul (and such a mystically inclined theologian as von Hügel thought that we could not say this), such absolute communications are at best rare and unpredictable flashes; and even where they seem to us to happen, are confined to the highest ranges of spiritual experience. They could never form its substance; and it would be an intolerable arrogance on our part — a departure from creatureliness bringing its own punishment with it — if we planned our inner life on such lines. We are sense-conditioned, and must use the senses in our approach to God; accepting the humbling truth that His absolute being is unknowable, and can only be apprehended by us under symbols and incarnational veils. This of course is both Christianity and common sense. But as well as this, we have to acknowledge that the real nature of His work within the soul is also unknowable by us. When we enter the phase of suffering, this truth becomes specially clear. Only by its transforming action within the mental or volitional life, purifying, illuminating, stirring to fervour or compelling to sacrifice, can we recognize the creative working of God. And even these inward experiences and acts, vital as they are for us, are still only symbolic in their conveyance of God. Récéjac's celebrated definition of mysticism, as "the tendency to approach the Absolute morally and by means of symbols," covers, when we properly understand it, the whole spiritual life of man; for the ground of the soul where His Spirit and our freedom meet, is beyond the reach of our direct perceptions. There is therefore no realistic religion for the human creature which is not expressed in symbolic acts. We cannot cut our world into two mutually exclusive parts and try to achieve the Infinite by a rejection of the finite. And when and if those more profound and really mystical depths of prayer are reached where we seem indeed to be subdued to a Presence and Action which has no image, and of which we can say nothing at all·— when the eternal background has become the eternal environment and we are sunk in God — then that very sense of an entire passivity which accompanies the soul's deepest action, of being, as Jacopone says, "drowned in the Divine Sea," is surely one more tribute to the part played by symbolism in the normal process of the spiritual life.

And at last, the essence of that life, *Dedication of the Will.* This of course is the ever-deeping temper of all personal religion worthy of the name. In its first movement it constitutes conversion; in its achieved perfection it is the very substance of the unitive life of the saint. But between those two points there is much work to be done and much suffering to be borne, by those in whom this self-transcendence, this supernatural growth, is taking place. Because of the primary importance of God's over-ruling action, and yet also the great importance of the self's free and willing activity, there must be within any full spiritual life, at least until its final stages, a constant tension between effort and abandonment, loving communion and ethical struggle, illumination and purification, renunciation of the will and deliberate use of the will: as the natural and supernatural aspects of personality, both invaded and subdued to the divine purpose, come into play, and the Will of God for that soul is expressed in calls to concrete activity, or to inward abandonment. So too in the actual life of prayer we ought to expect, and practise in some degree, both the deliberate effort of intercession and the abandoned quiet of contemplation. And as the soul grows in suppleness under these alternating stimulations — these "stirrings and touches of God," as the mystics so realistically call them — so its sense of the divine action, which is always there but not always recognized, becomes more distinct and individuated: until at last, in the full theopathetic life of the mystical saint, it becomes a perfectly responsive tool of the creative will. "I live yet not I." That of course is a real statement of experience, not a piece of piety: an experience which is reflected in the abnormal creative activities and spiritual power of the saints, from Paul of Tarsus to the Curé d'Ars.

And with this, I think, we reach the answer to the question with which we began: what exactly is the spiritual life? It is the life in which God and His eternal order have, more and more, their undivided sway; which is wholly turned to Him, devoted to Him, dependent on Him, and which at its term and commonly at the price of a long and costly struggle, makes the human creature a pure capacity for God. And as regards the actual prayer, the secret correspondence which accompanies this growth, this will tend mainly to fulfil itself along two paths: upwards to God in pure adoration — outward to the world in intercession. The interweaving of these two movements in the special way and degree in which they are developed by each soul, is the foundation of the spiritual life of man.

Meditation and Worship

Metropolitan Anthony Bloom

Metropolitan Anthony Bloom is the author of several excellent books about spirituality which combine genuinely helpful advice with a contemporary Orthodox theological perspective. He was trained as a physician in France and worked during World War Two with the Resistance. In 1943 he took secret monastic vows, and after his ordination in 1948 served as chaplain to the Fellowship of St. Alban and St. Sergius in London. Consecrated a bishop in 1958, he was made Archbishop of the Russian Orthodox Church in England and Ireland in 1962. His books include Living Prayer, Meditations, Beginning to Pray, God and Man, *and* Courage to Pray.

Meditation and prayer are often confused, but there is no danger in this confusion if meditation develops into prayer; only when prayer degenerates into meditation. Meditation primarily means thinking, even when God is the object of our thoughts. If as a result we gradually go deeper into a sense of worship and adoration, if the presence of God grows so powerful that we become aware of being with God, and if gradually, out of meditation we move into prayer, it is right; but the contrary should never be allowed, and in this respect there is a sharp difference between meditation and prayer.

The main distinction between meditation and our usual haphazard thinking is coherence; it should be an ascetical exercise of intellectual sobriety. Theophane the Recluse, speaking of the way in which people usually think, says that thoughts buzz around in our heads like a swarm of mosquitoes, in all directions, monotonously, without order and without particular result.

The first thing to learn, whatever the chosen subject of thought, is to pursue a line. Whenever we begin to think of God, of things divine, of anything that is the life of the soul, subsidiary thoughts appear; on every side we see so many possibilities, so many things that are full of interest and richness; but we must, having chosen the subject of our thinking, renounce all, except the chosen one. This is the only way in which our thoughts can be kept straight and can go deep.

The purpose of meditation is not to achieve an academic exercise in thinking; it is not meant to be a purely intellectual performance, nor a beautiful piece of thinking without further consequences; it is meant to be a piece of straight thinking under God's guidance and Godwards, and should lead us to draw conclusions about how to live. It is important to realise from the outset that a meditation has been useful when, as a result, it enables us to live more precisely and more concretely in accordance with the gospel.

Every one of us is impervious to certain problems and open to others; when we are not yet accustomed to thinking, it is better to begin with something which is alive for us, either with those sayings which we find attractive, which "make our heart burn within us," or else, on the contrary, with those against which we rebel, which we cannot accept; we find both in the gospel.

Whatever we take, a verse, a commandment, an event in the life of Christ, we must first of all assess its real objective content. This is extremely important because the purpose of meditation is not to build up a fantastic structure but to understand a truth. The truth is there, given, it is God's truth, and meditation is meant to be a bridge between our lack of understanding and the truth revealed. It is a way in which we can educate our intelligence, and gradually learn to have "the mind of Christ" as St Paul says (I Cor 2:16).

To make sure of the meaning of the text is not always as simple as it sounds; there are passages that are quite easy, there are other passages where words are used which can be understood only against the background of our experience, or of the traditional understanding of these words. For instance, the phrase "The Bride of the Lamb" can be understood only if we know what scripture means by the word "Lamb;" otherwise it becomes completely nonsensical and will be misunderstood. There are words which we can understand adequately only if we ignore the particular or technical meaning they may have acquired.

One such word is "spirit." For a christian, "spirit" is a technical word; it is either the Holy Spirit, the third person of the Trinity or one of the components of the human body — body and soul. It does not always convey with the same simplicity and breadth what the writers of the gospel meant to convey; it has become so specialised that it has lost contact with its root. To make sure of the text and what it means, there is also the definition given in the dictionary. The word spirit, or any other word, can be looked up and immediately seems simple and concrete, although it may have developed into a deeper meaning as a result of the efforts of theologians. But we should never start with the deepr meaning before we have got the simple concrete one, which everyone could understand at the time Christ spoke with the people around him.

There are things which we cannot understand except within the teaching of the Church; scripture must be understood with the mind of the Church, the mind of Christ, because the Church has not changed; in its inner experience it continues to live the same life as it lived in the first century; and words spoken by Paul, Peter, Basil or others within the Church, have kept their meaning. So, after a preliminary understanding in our own contemporary language, we must turn to what the Church means by the words; only then can we ascertain the meaning of the given text and have a right to start thinking and to draw conclusions. Once we have got the meaning of the text, we must see whether in its utter simplicity it does not already offer us suggestions, or even better, a straight command. As the aim of meditation, of understanding scripture, is to fulfil the will of God, we must draw practical conclusions and act upon them. When we have discovered the meaning, when in this sentence God has spoken to us, we must look into the matter and see what we can do, as in fact we do whenever we stumble on a good idea; when we come to realise that this or that is right, we immediately think how to integrate it into our life, in what way, on what occasion, by what method. It is not enough to understand what can be done and enthusiastically to start telling our friends all about it; we should start doing it. Paul the Simple, an Egyptian saint, once heard Anthony the Great read the first verse of the first Psalm: "Blessed is the man that walketh not in the counsel of the ungodly," and immediately, Paul departed into the wilderness. Only after some thirty years, when Anthony met him again, St. Paul said to him with great humility: "I have spent all this time trying to become the man that does not walk in the counsel of the ungodly." We do not need understanding on many points to reach perfection; what we need is thirty years of work to try to understand and to become that new man.

Often we consider one or two points and jump to the next, which is wrong since we have just seen that it takes a long time to become recollected, what the Fathers call an attentive person, someone capable of paying attention to an idea so long and so well that nothing of it is lost. The spiritual writers of the past and of the present day will all tell us: take a text, ponder on it hour after hour, day after day, until you have exhausted all your possibilities, intellectual and emotional, and thanks to attentive reading and re-reading of this text, you have to come to a new attitude. Quite often meditation consists in nothing but examining the text, turning over these words of God addressed to us, so as to become completely familiar with them, so imbued with them that gradually we and these words become completely one. In this process, even if we think that we have not found any particular intellectual richness, we have changed.

On many occasions we can do a lot of thinking; there are plenty of situations in our daily life in which we have nothing to do except wait, and if we are disciplined — and this is part of our spiritual training — we will be able to concentrate quickly and fix our attention at once on the subject of our thoughts, of our meditation. We must learn to do it by compelling our thoughts to attach themselves to one focus and to drop everything else. In the beginning, extraneous thoughts will intrude, but if we push them away constantly, time after time, in the end they will leave us in peace. It is only when by training, by exercise, by habit, we have become able to concentrate profoundly and quickly, that we can continue through life in a state of collectedness, in spite of what we are doing. However, to become aware of having extraneous thoughts, we must already have achieved some sort of collectedness. We can be in a crowd, surrounded by people and yet completely alone and untouched by what is going on; it depends on us whether to allow what is happening outside to become an event in our inner life or not; if we allow it to, our attention will break down, but if we do not, we can be completely isolated and collected in God's presence whatever happens around us. There is a story by Al Absihi about this sort of concentration. A Moslem's family used to keep a respectful silence whenever he had a visitor, but they knew that they could make as much noise as they wanted while he was praying, because at such times he heard nothing; in fact, one day he was not even disturbed by a fire that broke out in his house.

We may sometimes find ourselves in a group of people arguing hotly with no hope of a solution. We cannot leave without causing further disorder, but what we can do is mentally to withdraw, turn to Christ and say, "I know that you are here, help!" And just be with Christ. If it did not sound so absurd one would say, make

Christ present in the situation. Objectively he is always present, but there is some difference between being there objectively and being introduced by an act of faith into a given situation. One can do nothing but sit back and just remain with Christ and let the others talk. His presence will do more than anything one could say. And from time to time, in an unexpected way, if one keeps quiet and silent together with Christ, one will discover that one can say something quite sensible that would have been impossible in the heat of argument.

Parallel with mental discipline, we must learn to acquire a peaceful body. Whatever our psychological activity, our body reacts to it; and our bodily state determines to a certain degree the type or quality of our psychological activity. Theophane the Recluse, in his advice to anyone wishing to attempt the spiritual life, says that one of the conditions indispensable to success is never to permit bodily slackness: "Be like a violin string, tuned to a precise note, without slackness or supertension, the body erect, shoulders back, carriage of the head easy, the tension of all muscles oriented towards the heart." A great deal has been written and said about the ways in which one can make use of the body to increase one's ability to be attentive, but on a level accessible to many, Theophane's advice seems to be simple, precise and practical. We must learn to relax and be alert at the same time. We must master our body so that it should not intrude but make collectedness easier for us.

Meditation is an activity of thought, while prayer is the rejection of every thought. According to the teaching of the eastern Fathers, even pious thoughts and the deepest and loftiest theological considerations, if they occur during prayer, must be considered as a temptation and suppressed; because, as the Fathers say, it is foolish to think about God and forget that you are in his presence. All the spiritual guides of Orthodoxy warn us against replacing this meeting with God by thinking about him. Prayer is essentially standing face to face with God, consciously striving to remain collected and absolutely still and attentive in his presence, which means standing with an undivided mind, an undivided heart and an undivided will in the presence of the Lord; and that is not easy. Whatever our training may give us, there is always a short cut open at any time: undividedness can be attained by the person for whom the love of God is everything, who has broken all ties, who is completely given to God; then there is no longer personal striving, but the working of the radiant grace of God.

God must always be the focus of our attention for there are many ways in which the collectedness may be falsified; when we pray from a deep concern, we have a sense that our whole being has become one prayer and we imagine that we have been in a state of deep, real prayerful collectedness, but this is not true, because the focus of attention was not God; it was the object of our prayers. When we are emotionally involved, no alien thought intrudes, because we are completely concerned with what we are praying about; it is only when we turn to pray for some other person or need that our attention is suddenly dispersed, which means that it was not the thought of God, not the sense of his presence that was the cause of this concentration, but our human concern. It does not mean that human concern is of no importance, but it means that the thought of a friend can do more than the thought of God, which is a serious point.

One of the reasons why we find it so difficult to be attentive is that the act of faith which we make in affirming: "God is here," carries too little weight for us. We are intellectually aware that God is here, but not aware of it physically in a way that would collect and focus all our energies, thoughts, emotions and will, making us nothing but attention. If we prepare for prayer by a process of imagination: "The Lord Christ is here, that is what he looks like, this is what I know about him, this is what he means to me ...," the richer the image, the less real the presence, because it is an idol that is built which obscures the real presence. We can derive some help from it for a sort of emotional concentration, but it is not God's presence, the real, objective presence of God.

The early Fathers and the whole Orthodox tradition teach us that we must concentrate, by an effort of will, on the words of the prayer we pronounce. We must pronounce the words attentively, matter-of-factly, without trying to create any sort of emotional state, and we must leave it to God to arouse whatever response we are capable of.

St. John Climacus gives us a simple way of learning to concentrate. He says: choose a prayer, be it the Lord's Prayer or any other, take your stand before God, become aware of where you are and what you are doing, and pronounce the words of the prayer attentively. After a certain time you will discover that your thoughts have wandered; then restart the prayer on the words or the sentence which was the last you pronounced attentively. You may have to do that ten times, twenty times or fifty times; you may, in the time appointed for your prayer, be able to pronounce only three sentences, three petitions and go no farther; but in this struggle you will have been able to concentrate on the words, so that you bring to God, seriously, soberly, respectfully, words of prayer which you are conscious of, and not an offering that is not yours, because you were not aware of it.

John Climacus also advises us to read the prayer of our choice without haste, in a monotonous way, slowly enough to have time to pay attention to the words, but not so slowly as to make the exercise dull; and to do it without trying to experience anything emotionally, because what we aim at is a relationship with God. We should never try to squeeze out of the heart any sort of feeling when we come to God; a prayer is a statement, the rest depends on God.

In this way of training a given amount of time is set apart for prayer, and if prayer is attentive, it does not matter what this length of time is. If you were meant to read three pages in your rule of prayer and saw that after half an hour you were still reading the first twelve words, of course it would raise a feeling of discouragement; therefore, the best way is to have a definite time and keep to it. You know the time fixed and you have the prayer material to make use of; if you struggle earnestly, quite soon you will discover that your attention becomes docile, because the attention is much more subject to the will than we imagine, and when one is absolutely sure that however one tries to escape, it must be twenty minutes and not a quarter of an hour, one just perseveres. St. John Climacus trained dozens of monks by this simple device — a time limit, then merciless attention, and that is all.

The outward beauty of the liturgy must not seduce us into forgetting that sobriety in prayer is a very important feature in Orthodoxy. In the *Way of a Pilgrim* a village priest gives some very authoritative advice on prayer: "If you want it to be pure, right and enjoyable, you must choose some short prayer, consisting of few but forcible words, and repeat it frequently, over a long period. Then you find delight in prayer." The same idea is to be found in the *Letters of Brother Lawrence*: "I do not advise you to use multiplicity of words in prayer; many words and long discourses being often the occasions of wandering."

John of Kronstadt was asked once how it was that priests, in spite of their training, experience wandering, intrusive thoughts, even in the course of the liturgy. The answer was: "Because of our lack of faith." We have not faith enough, faith being understood in the terms of St. Paul as "the evidence of things not seen" (Heb 11:1). But it would be a mistake to think that those distracting thoughts all come from outside; we must face the fact that they come from our own depths: they are our continual inner preoccupations coming to the fore, they are just the thoughts that usually fill our life, and the only way to get radically rid of unworthy thoughts is to change our outlook on life fundamentally. Again, as Brother Lawrence puts it in his eighth letter: "One way to recollect the mind easily in the time of prayer, and preserve it more in tranquility, is not to let it wander too far at other times; you should keep it strictly in the presence of God; and being accustomed to think of him often, you will find it easy to keep your mind calm at the time of prayer, or at least to recall it from its wanderings."

As long as we care deeply for all the trivialities of life, we cannot hope to pray wholeheartedly; they will always colour the train of our thoughts. The same is true about our daily relations with other people, which should not consist merely of gossip but be based on what is essential in every one of us, otherwise we may find ourselves unable to reach another level when we turn to God. We must eradicate everything meaningless and trivial in ourselves and in our relations with others, and concentrate on those things we shall be able to take with us into eternity.

It is not possible to become another person the moment we start to pray, but by keeping watch on one's thoughts one learns gradually to differentiate their value. It is in our daily life that we cultivate the thoughts which irrepressibly spring up at the time of prayer. Prayer in its turn will change and enrich our daily life, becoming the foundation of a new and real relationship with God and those around us.

In our struggle for prayer the emotions are almost irrelevant; what we must bring to God is a complete, firm determination to be faithful to him and strive that God should live in us. We must remember that the fruits of prayer are not this or that emotional state, but a deep change in the whole of our personality. What we aim at is to be made able to stand before God and to concentrate on his presence, all our needs being directed Godwards, and to be given power, strength, anything we need that the will of God may be fulfilled in us. That the will of God should be fulfilled in us is the only aim of prayer, and it is also the criterion of right prayer. It is not the mystical feeling we may have, or our emotions that make good praying. Theophane the Recluse says: "You ask yourself, 'Have I prayed well today?' Do not try to find out how deep your emotions were, or how much deeper you understand things divine; ask yourself: 'Am I doing God's will better than I did before?' If you are, prayer has brought its fruit, if you are not, it has not, whatever amount of understanding or feeling you may have derived from the time spent in the presence of God."

Concentration whether in meditation or in prayer, can only be achieved by an effort of will. Our spiritual life is based on our faith and determination, and any incidental joys are a gift of God. St. Seraphim of Sarov, when asked what it was that made some people remain sinners and never make any progress while others were becoming saints and living in God, answered: "Only determination." Our activities must be determined by an act of will, which usually happens to be contrary to what we long for; this will, based on our faith, always clashes with another will, our instinctive one. There are two wills in us, one is the conscious will, possessed to a greater or lesser degree, which consists in the ability to compel ourselves to act in accordance with our convictions. The second one is something else in us, it is the longings, the claims, the desires of all our nature, quite often contrary to the first will. St. Paul speaks of two laws that fight against each other (Rom 7:23). He speaks of the old and the new Adam in us, who are at war. We know that one must die in order that the other should live, and we must realize that our spiritual life, our life as a human being taken as a whole, will never be complete as long as these two wills do not coincide. It is not enough to aim at the victory of the good will against the evil one; the evil one, that is the longings of our fallen nature, must absolutely, though gradually, be transformed into a longing, a craving for God. The struggle is hard and far-reaching.

The spiritual life, the christian life does not consist in developing a strong will capable of compelling us to do what we do not want. In a sense, of course, it is an achievement to do the right things when we really wish to do the wrong ones, but it remains a small achievement. A mature spiritual life implies that our conscious will is in accordance with the words of God and has remoulded, transformed our nature so deeply, with the help of God's grace, that the totality of our human person is only one will. To begin with, we must submit and curb our will into obedience to the commandments of Christ, taken objectively, even when they clash with what we know about life. We must, in an act of faith, admit against the evidence that Christ is right. Experience teaches us that certain things do not seem to work as the gospels say they should; but God says they do, so they must. We must also remember that when we fulfil God's will in this objective sense, we must not do it tentatively, thinking of putting it to the test, to see what comes of it, because then it does not work. Experience teaches us that when we are slapped on one cheek, we want to retaliate; Christ says "turn the other cheek." What we really expect when we finally determine to turn the other cheek is to convert the enemy and win his admiration. But when instead we are slapped again, we are usually surprised or indignant, as though God has cheated us into doing something quite un-workable.

We must outgrow this attitude, be prepared to do God's will and pay the cost. Unless we are prepared to pay the cost, we are wasting our time. Then, as a next step, we must learn that doing is not enough, because we must not be drilled into christianity, but we must *become* christians; we must learn, in the process of doing the will of God, to understand God's purpose. Christ has made his intentions clear to us and it is not in vain that in St John's gospel he no longer calls us servants but friends, because the servant does not know the mind of the master, and he has told us all things (Jn 15:15). We must, by doing the will of God, learn what this doing implies, so that in thought, in will, in attitude, we may become co-workers with Christ (I Cor 3:9). Being of one mind we shall gradually become inwardly what we try to be outwardly.

We see that we cannot partake deeply of the life of God unless we change profoundly. It is therefore essential that we should go to God in order that he should transform and change us, and that is why, to begin with we should ask for conversion. Conversion in Latin means a turn, a change in the direction of things. The Greek word *metanoia* means a change of mind. Conversion means that instead of spending our lives looking in all directions, we should follow one direction only. It is a turning away from a great many things which we valued solely because they were pleasant or expedient for us. The first impact of conversion is to modify our sense of values: God being at the centre of all, everything acquires a new position and a new depth. All that is God's, all that belongs to him, is positive and real. Everything that is outside him has no value or meaning. But it is not a change of mind alone that we can call conversion. We can change our minds and go no farther; what must follow is an act of will and unless our will comes into motion and is redirected Godwards, there is no conversion; at most there is only an incipient, still dormant and inactive change in us. Obviously it is not enough to look in the right direction and never move. Repentance must not be mistaken for remorse, it does not consist in feeling terribly sorry that things went wrong in the past; it is an active, positive attitude which consists in moving in the right direction. It is made very clear in the parable of the two sons (Mt 21:28) who were commanded by their father to go to work at his vineyard. The one said, "I am going," but did not go. The other said, "I am not going," and then felt ashamed and went to work. This was real repentance, and we should never lure ourselves into imagining that to lament one's past is an act of repentance. It is part of it of course, but repentance remains unreal and barren as long as it has not led us to doing the will of the father. We have a tendency to think that it should result in fine emotions and we are quite often satisfied with emotions instead of real, deep changes.

When we have hurt someone and realise that we were wrong, quite often we go and express our sorrow to the person, and when the conversation has been emotionally tense, when there were a lot of tears and forgiveness and moving words, we go away with a sense of having done everything possible. We have wept together, we are at peace and now everything is all right. It is not all right at all. We have simply delighted in our virtues and the other person, who may be goodhearted and easily moved, has reacted to our emotional scene. But this is just what conversion is not. No one asks us to shed tears, nor to have a touching encounter with the victim, even when the victim is God. What is expected is that having understood the wrong, we should put it right.

Nor does conversion end there; it must lead us farther in the process of making us different. Conversion begins but it never ends. It is an increasing process in which we gradually become more and more what we should be, until, after the day of judgement, these categories of fall, conversion and righteousness disappear and are replaced by new categories of a new life. As Christ says: "I make all things new" (Rev 21:5).

One can pray everywhere and anywhere, yet there are places where prayer finds its natural climate; those places are churches, fulfilling the promise; "I will make them joyful in my house of prayer" (Is 56:7).

A church, once consecrated, once set part, becomes the dwelling-place of God. He is present there in another way than in the rest of the world. In the world he is present as a stranger, as a pilgrim, as one who goes from door to door, who has nowhere to rest his head; he goes as the lord of the world who has been rejected by the world and expelled from his kingdom and who has returned to it to save his people. In church he is at home, it is his place; he is not only the creator and the lord by right but he is recognised as such. Outside it he acts when he can and how he can; inside a church he has all power and all might and it is for us to come to him.

When we build a church or set apart a place of worship we do something which reaches far beyond the obvious significance of the fact. The whole world which God created has become a place where men have sinned; the devil has been at work, a fight is going on constantly; there is no place on this earth which has not been soiled by blood, suffering or sin. When we choose a minute part of it, calling upon the power of God himself, in rites which convey his grace, to bless it, when we cleanse it from the presence of the evil spirit and set it apart to be God's foothold on earth, we reconquer for God a small part of this desecrated world. We may say that this is a place where the kingdom of God reveals itself and manifests itself with power. When we come to church we should be aware that we are entering upon sacred ground, a place which belongs to God, and we should behave accordingly.

The icons seen on church walls are not merely images or paintings: an icon is a focus of real presence. St. John Chrysostom advises us, before we start praying, to take our stand in front of an icon and to shut our eyes. He says "shut your eyes," because it is not by examining the icon, by using it as a visual aid, that we are helped by it to pray. It is not a substantial presence in the sense in which the bread and wine are the body and blood of Christ. An icon is not, in this sense, Christ, but there is a mysterious link between the two. By the power of grace an icon participates in something which can best be defined in the words of Gregory Palamas as the energies of Christ, as the active power of Christ working for our salvation.

An icon is painted as an act of worship. The wood is chosen and blessed, the paint is blessed, the man who wishes to paint prepares himself by fasting, by confession, by communion. He keeps ascetical rules while working and when his work is completed, it is blessed with holy water and chrismated (this last part of the blessing is now often omitted, unfortunately). Thus, by the power of the Holy Spirit, the icon becomes more than a painting. It is loaded with presence, imbued with the grace of the Spirit and linked with the particular saint it represents in and through the mystery of the communion of saints and the cosmic unity of all things. One cannot say of the icon that the indwelling of the saint is identical with or even similar to that which we find in the holy gifts, and yet it is a focus of real presence as it is experienced and taught by the Church. An icon is not a likeness, it is a sign. Certain icons have been singled out by the power and wisdom of God to be miraculous icons. When you stand in their presence you feel challenged by them.

A priest who visited Russia recently took services in a church where there was a well-known wonder-working icon of Our Lady and was deeply conscious of her active participation in the service. The icon had become very dark in the course of centuries, and from the place where he stood he could not distinguish the features, so he continued to celebrate with his eyes shut. Suddenly he felt that the Mother of God in the icon was as it were compelling him to pray, directing his prayers, shaping his mind. He became aware of a power originating from the icon that filled the church with prayer and guided the diffuse thoughts. It was almost a physical presence, there was a person standing there, compelling a response.

The Spiritual Father in Orthodox Christianity

Kallistos Ware

Kallistos Ware is Bishop of Diokleia and Spalding Lecturer in Eastern Orthodox Studies at Oxford University. He is the first Englishman to be made a bishop of the Greek Orthodox Church. Bishop Kallistos is the author of several books, the best known of which is The Orthodox Church, *one of the best introductions to Orthodoxy. Here he explores the role of the* starets — *the spiritual father* — *in Eastern Christian tradition.*

One who climbs a mountain for the first time needs to follow a known route; and he needs to have with him, as companion and guide, someone who has been up before and is familiar with the way. To serve as such a companion and guide is precisely the role of the "Abba" or spiritual father — whom the Greeks call "Geron" and the Russians "Starets," a title which in both languages means "old man" or "elder."[1]

The importance of obedience to a *Geron* is underlined from the first emergence of monasticism in the Christian East. St. Antony of Egypt said "I know of monks who fell after much toil and lapsed into madness, because they trusted in their own work ... So far as possible, for every step that a monk takes, for every drop of water that he drinks in his cell, he should entrust the decision to the Old Men, to avoid making some mistake in what he does."[2]

This is a theme constantly emphasized in the *Apophthegmata* or *Sayings of the Desert Fathers:* "The old Men used to say: 'if you see a young monk climbing up to heaven by his own will, grasp him by the feet and throw him down, for this is to his profit ... if a man has faith in another and renders himself up to him in full submission, he has no need to attend to the commandment of God, but he needs only to entrust his entire will into the hands of his father. Then he will be blameless before God, for God requires nothing from beginners so much as self-stripping through obedience.' "[3]

This figure of the *Starets*, so prominent in the first generations of Egyptian monasticism, has retained its full significance up to the present day in Orthodox Christendom. "There is one thing more important than all possible books and ideas," states a Russian layman of the 19th Century, the Slavophile Kireyevsky, "and that is the example of an Orthodox *Starets*, before whom you can lay each of your thoughts and from whom you can hear, not a more or less valuable private opinion, but the judgement of the Holy Fathers. God be praised, such *Startsi* have not yet disappeared from our Russia." And a priest of the Russian emigration in our own century, Fr. Alexander Elchaninov (†1934), writes: "Their field of action is unlimited ... they are undoubtedly saints, recognized as such by the people. I feel that in our tragic days it is precisely through this means that faith will survive and be strengthened in our country."[4]

What entitles a man to act as a starets? How and by whom is he appointed?

To this there is a simple answer. The spiritual father or starets is essentially a "charismatic" and prophetic figure, accredited for his task by the direct action of the Holy Spirit. He is ordained, not by the hand of man, but by the hand of God. He is an expression of the Church as "event" or "happening," rather than of the Church as institution.[5]

There is, of course, no sharp line of demarcation between the prophetic and the institutional in the life of the Church; each grows out of the other and is intertwined with it. The ministry of the starets, itself charismatic, is related to a clearly-defined function within the institutional framework of the Church, the office of priest-confessor. In the Eastern Orthodox tradition, the right to hear confessions is not granted automatically at ordination. Before acting as confessor, a priest requires authorization from his bishop; in the Greek Church, only a minority of the clergy are so authorized.

Although the sacrament of confession is certainly an appropriate occasion for spiritual direction, the ministry of the starets is not identical with that of a confessor. The starets gives advice, not only at confession, but on many other occasions; indeed, while the confessor must always be a priest, the starets may be a simple monk, not in holy orders, or a nun, a layman or laywoman. The ministry of the starets is deeper, because only a very few confessor priests would claim to speak with the former's insight and authority.

But if the starets is not ordained or appointed by an act of the official hierarchy, how does he come to embark on his ministry? Sometimes an existing starets will designate his own successor. In this way, at certain monastic centers such as Optina in 19th century Russia, there was established an "apostolic succession" of spiritual masters. In other cases, the starets simply emerges spontaneously, without any act of external authorization. As Elchaninov said, they are "recognized as such by the people." Within the continuing life of the Christian community, it becomes plain to the believing people of God (the true guardian of Holy Tradition) that this or that person has the gift of spiritual fatherhood. Then, in a free and informal fashion, others begin to come to him or her for advice and direction.

It will be noted that the initiative comes, as a rule, not from the master but from the disciples. It would be perilously presumptuous for someone to say in his own heart or to others, "Come and submit yourselves to me; I am a starets, I have the grace of the Spirit." What happens, rather, is that — without any claims being made by the starets himself — others approach him, seeking his advice or asking to live permanently under his care. At first, he will probably send them away, telling them to consult someone else. Finally the moment comes when he no longer sends them away but accepts their coming to him as a disclosure of the will of God. Thus it is his spiritual children who reveal the starets to himself.

The figure of the starets illustrates the two interpenetrating levels on which the earthly Church exists and functions. On the one hand, there is the external, official, and hierarchial level, with its geographical organization into dioceses and parishes, its great centers (Rome, Constantinople, Moscow, and Canterbury), and its "apostolic succession" of bishops. On the other hand, there is the inward, spiritual and "charismatic" level, to which the startsi primarily belong. Here the chief centers are, for the most part, not the great primatial and metropolitan sees, but certain remote hermitages, in which there shine forth a few personalities richly endowed with spiritual gifts. Most startsi have possessed no exalted status in the formal hierarchy of the Church; yet the influence of a simple priest-monk such as St. Seraphim of Sarov has exceeded that of any patriarch or bishop in 19th century Orthodoxy. In this fashion, alongside the apostolic succession of the episcopate, there exists that of the saints and spiritual men. Both types of succession are essential for the true functioning of the Body of Christ, and it is through their interaction that the life of the Church on earth is accomplished.

Although the starets is not ordained or appointed for his task, it is certainly necessary that he sould be *prepared*. The classic pattern for this preparation, which consists in a movement of flight and return, may be clearly discerned in the lives of St. Antony of Egypt (†356) and St. Seraphim of Sarov (†1833).

St. Antony's life falls sharply into two halves, with his fifty-fifth year as the watershed. The years from early manhood to the age of fifty-five were his time of preparation, spent in an ever-increasing seclusion from the world as he withdrew further and further into the desert. He eventually passed twenty years in an abandoned fort, meeting no one whatsoever. When he had reached the age of fifty-five, his friends could contain their curiosity no longer, and broke down the entrance. St. Antony came out and, for the remaining half century of his long life, without abandoning the life of a hermit, he made himself freely available to others, acting as "a physician given by God to Egypt." He was beloved by all, adds his biographer, St. Athanasius, "and all desired to have him as their father."[6] Observe that the transition from enclosed anchorite to spiritual father came about, not through any initiative on St. Antony's part, but through the action of others. Antony was a lay monk, never ordained to the priesthood.

St. Seraphim followed a comparable path. After fifteen years spent in the ordinary life of the monastic community, as novice, professed monk, deacon, and priest, he withdrew for thirty years of solitude and almost total silence. During the first part of this period he lived in a forest hut; at one point he passed a thousand days on the stump of a tree and a thousand nights of those days on a rock, devoting himself to unceasing prayer. Recalled by his abbot to the monastery, he obeyed the order without the slightest delay; and during the latter part of his time of solitude he lived rigidly enclosed in his cell, which he did not leave even to attend services in church; on Sundays the priest brought communion to him at the door of his room. Though he was a priest he didn't celebrate the liturgy. Finally, in the last eight years of his life, he ended his enclosure, opening the door of his cell and receiving all who came. He did nothing to advertise himself or to summon people; it was the others who took the initiative in approaching him, but when they came — sometimes hundreds or even thousands in a single day — he did not send them empty away.

Without this intense ascetic preparation, without this radical flight into solitude, could St. Antony or St. Seraphim have acted in the same degree as guide to those of their generation? Not that they withdrew *in order* to become masters and guides of others. They fled, not in order to prepare themselves for some other task, but out of a consuming desire to be alone with God. God accepted their love, but then sent them back as instruments of healing in the world from which they had withdrawn. Even had He never sent them back, their flight would still have been supremely creative and valuable to society; for the monk helps the world not primarily by anything that he does and says but by what he *is*, by the state of unceasing prayer which has become identical with his innermost being. Had St. Antony and St. Seraphim done nothing but pray in solitude they would still have been serving their fellow men to the highest degree. As things turned out, however, God ordained that they should also serve others in a more direct fashion. But this direct and visible service was essentially a consequence of the invisible service which they rendered through their prayer.

"Acquire inward peace," said St. Seraphim, "and a multitude of men around you will find their salvation."[7] Such is the role of spiritual fatherhood. Establish yourself in God; then you can bring others to His presence. A man must learn to be alone, he must listen in the stillness of his own heart to the wordless speech of the Spirit, and so discover the truth about himself and God. Then his work to others will be a word of power, because it is a word out of silence.

What Nikos Kazantzakis said of the almond tree is true also of the starets:

> "I said to the almond tree,
> 'Sister, speak to me of God,'
> And the almond tree blossomed."

Shaped by the encounter with God in solitude, the starets is able to heal by his very presence. He guides and forms others, not primarily by words of advice, but by his companionship, by the living and specific example which he sets — in a word, by blossoming like the almond tree. He teaches as much by his silence as by his speech. "Abba Theophilus the Archbishop once visited Scetis, and when the brethren had assembled they said to Abba Pambo, 'Speak a word to the Pope that he may be edified.' The Old Man said to them, 'if he is not edified by my silence neither will be he edified by my speech.' "[8] A story with the same moral is told of St. Antony. "It was the custom of three Fathers to visit the Blessed Antony once each year, and two of them used to ask him questions about their thoughts (logismoi) and the salvation of their soul; but the third remained completely silent, without putting any questions. After a long while, Abba Antony said to him, 'See, you have been in the habit of coming to me all this time, and yet you do not ask me any questions.' And the other replied, 'Father, it is enough for me just to look at you.' "[9]

The real journey of the starets is not spatially into the desert, but spiritually into the heart. External solitude, while helpful, is not indispensible, and a man may learn to stand alone before God, while yet continuing to pursue a life of active service in the midst of society. St. Antony of Egypt was told that a doctor in Alexandria was his equal in spiritual achievement: "In the city there is someone like you, a doctor by profession, who gives all his money to the needy, and the whole day long he sings the Thrice-Holy Hymn with the angels."[10] We are not told how this revelation came to Antony, nor what was the name of the doctor, but one thing is clear. Unceasing prayer of the heart is no monopoly of the solitaries; the mystical and "angelic" life is possible in the city as well as the desert. The Alexandrian doctor accomplished the inward journey without severing his outward links with the community.

There are also many instances in which flight and return are not sharply distinguished in temporal sequence. Take, for example, the case of St. Seraphim's younger contemporary, Bishop Ignaty Brianchaninov (✝1867). Trained originally as an army officer, he was appointed at the early age of twenty-six to take charge of a busy and influential monastery close to St. Petersburg. His own monastic training had lasted little more than four years before he was placed in a position of authority. After twenty-four years as Abbot, he was consecrated Bishop. Four years later he resigned, to spend the remaining six years of his life as a hermit. Here a period of active pastoral work preceded the period of anachoretic seclusion. When he was made abbot, he must surely have felt gravely ill-prepared. His secret withdrawal into the heart was undertaken continuously during the many years in which he administered a monastery and a diocese; but it did not receive an exterior expression until the very end of his life.[11]

Bishop Ignaty's career may serve as a paradigm to many of us at the present time, although (needless to say) we fall far short of his level of spiritual achievement. Under the pressure of outward circumstances and probably without clearly realizing what is happening to us, we become launched on a career of teaching, preaching, and pastoral counselling, while lacking any deep knowledge of the desert and its creative silence. But through teaching others we ourselves begin to learn. Slowly we recognize our powerlessness to heal the wounds of humanity solely through philanthropic programs, common sense, and psychiatry. Our complacency is broken down, we appreciate our own inadequacy, and start to understand what Christ meant by the "one thing that is necessary" (Luke 10:42). That is the moment when we enter upon the path of the starets. Through our pastoral experience, through our anguish over the pain of others, we are brought to undertake the journey inwards, to ascend the secret ladder of the Kingdom, where alone a genuine solution to the world's problems can be found. No doubt few if any among us would think of ourselves as a starets in the full sense, but provided we seek with humble sincerity to enter into the "secret chamber" of our heart, we can all share to some degree in the grace of the spiritual fatherhood. Perhaps we shall never outwardly lead the life of a monastic recluse or a hermit — that rests with God — but what is supremely important is that each should see the need to be a hermit of the heart.

Three gifts in particular distinguish the spiritual father. The first is *insight and discernment* (diakrisis), the ability to perceive intuitively the secrets of another's heart, to understand the hidden depths of which the other is unaware. The spiritual father penetrates beneath the conventional gestures and attitudes whereby we conceal our true personality from others and from ourselves; and, beyond all these trivialities, he comes to grips with the unique person made in the image and likeness of God. This power is spiritual rather than psychic; it is not simply a kind of extra-sensory perception or a sanctified clairvoyance but the fruit of grace, presupposing concentrated prayer and an unremitting ascetic struggle.

With this gift of insight there goes the ability to use words with power. As each person comes before him, the starets knows — immediately and specifically — what it is that the individual needs to hear. Today, we are inundated with words, but for the most part these are conspicuously *not* words uttered with power.[12] The starets uses few words, and sometimes none at all; but by these few words or by his silence, he is able to alter the whole direction of a man's life. At Bethany, Christ used three words only: "Lazarus, come out" (John 11:43) and these three words, spoken with power, were sufficient to bring the dead back to life. In an age when language has been disgracefully trivialized, it is vital to rediscover the power of the word; and this means rediscovering the nature of silence, not just as a pause between words but as one of the primary realities of existence. Most teachers and preachers talk far too much; the starets is distinguished by an austere economy of language.

But for a word to possess power, it is necessary that there should be not only one who speaks with the genuine authority of personal experience, but also one who listens with attention and eagerness. If someone questions a starets out of idle curiosity, it is likely that he will receive little benefit; but if he approaches the starets with ardent faith and deep hunger, the word that he hears may transfigure his being. The words of the startsi are for the most part simple in verbal expression and devoid of literary artifice; to those who read them in a superficial way, they will seem jejune and banal.

The spiritual father's gift of insight is exercised primarily through the practice known as "disclosure of thoughts" (*logismois*). In early Eastern monasticism the young monk used to go daily to his father and lay before him all the thoughts which had come to him during the day. This disclosure of thoughts includes far more than a confession of sins, since the novice also speaks of those ideas and impulses which may seem innocent to him, but in which the spiritual father may discern secret dangers or significant signs. Confession is retrospective, dealing with sins that have already occurred; the disclosure of thoughts, on the other hand, is prophylactic, for it lays bare our logismoi before they have led to sin and so deprives them of their power to harm. The purpose of the disclosure is not juridical, to secure absolution from guilt, but self-knowledge, that each may see himself as he truly is.[13]

Endowed with discernment, the spiritual father does not merely wait for a person to reveal himself, but shows to the other thoughts hidden from him. When people came to St. Seraphim of Sarov, he often answered their difficulties before they had time to put their thoughts before him. On many occasions the answer at first seemed quite irrelevant, and even absurd and irresponsible; for what St. Seraphim answered was not the question his visitor had consciously in mind, but the one he ought to have been asking. In all this St. Seraphim relied on the inward light of the Holy Spirit. He found it important, he explained, not to work out in advance what he was going to say; in that case, his words would represent merely his own human judgment, which might well be in error, and not the judgment of God.

In St. Seraphim's eyes, the relationship between starets and spiritual child is stronger than death, and he therefore urged his children to continue their disclosure of thoughts to him even after his departure to the next life. These are the words which, by his own command, were written on his tomb: "When I am dead, come to me at my grave, and the more often, the better. Whatever is on your soul, whatever may have happened to you, come to me as when I was alive and, kneeling on the ground, cast all your bitterness upon my grave. Tell me everything and I shall listen to you, and all the bitterness will fly away from you. And as you spoke to me when I was alive, do so now. For I am living, and I shall be forever."

The second gift of the spiritual father is *the ability to love others and to make others' sufferings his own*. Of Abba Poemen, one of the greatest of the Egyptian gerontes, it is briefly and simply recorded: "He possessed love, and many came to him."[14] *He possessed love* — this is indispensable in all spiritual fatherhood. Unlimited insight into the secrets of men's hearts, if devoid of loving compassion, would not be creative but destructive; he who cannot love others will have little power to heal them.

Loving others involves suffering with and for them; such is the literal sense of compassion. "Bear one another's burdens, and so fulfill the law of Christ" (Galatians 6:2). The spiritual father is the one who *par excellence* bears the burdens of others. "A starets," writes Dostoevsky in *The Brothers Karamazov*, "is one who takes your soul, your will, unto his soul and his will ..." It is not enough for him to offer advice. He is also required to take up the soul of his spiritual children into his own soul, their life into his life. It is his task to pray for them, and his constant intercession on their behalf is more important to them than any words of counsel.[15] It is his task likewise to assume their sorrows and their sins, to take their guilt upon himself, and to answer for them at the Last Judgment.

All this is manifest in a primary document of Eastern spiritual direction, the *Books of Varsanuphius and John*, embodying some 850 questions addressed to two elders of 6th-century Palestine, together with their written answers. "As God Himself knows," Varsanuphius insists to his spiritual children, "there is not a second or an hour when I do not have you in my mind and in my prayers ... I care for you more than you care for yourself ... I would gladly lay down my life for you." This is his prayer to God: "O Master, either bring my children with me into Your Kingdom, or else wipe me also out of Your book." Taking up the theme of bearing others' burdens, Varsanuphius affirms: "I am bearing your burdens and your offences ... You have become like a man sitting under a shady tree ... I take upon myself the sentence of condemnation against you, and by the grace of Christ, I will not abandon you, either in this age or in the Age to Come."[16]

47

Readers of Charles Williams will be reminded of the principle of "substituted love," which plays a central part in *Descent into Hell.* The same line of thought is expressed by Dostoevsky's starets Zosima: "There is only one way of salvation, and that is to make yourself responsible for all men's sins ... To make yourself responsible in all sincerity for everything and for everyone." The ability of the starets to support and strengthen others is measured by his willingness to adopt this way of salvation.

Yet the relation between the spiritual father and his children is not one-sided. Though he takes the burden of their guilt upon himself and answers for them before God, he cannot do this effectively unless they themselves are struggling wholeheartedly for their own salvation. Once a brother came to St. Antony of Egypt and said: "Pray for me." But the Old Man replied: "Neither will I take pity on you nor will God, unless you make some effort of your own."[17]

When considering the love of a starets for those under his care, it is important to give full meaning to the word "father" in the title "spiritual father". As father and offspring in an ordinary family should be joined in mutual love, so it must also be within the "charismatic" family of the starets. It is primarily a relationship in the Holy Spirit, and while the wellspring of human affection is not to be unfeelingly suppressed, it must be contained within bounds. It is recounted how a young monk looked after his elder, who was gravely ill, for twelve years without interruption. Never once in that period did his elder thank him or so much as speak one word of kindness to him. Only on his death-bed did the Old Man remark to the assembled brethren, "He is an angel and not a man."[18] The story is valuable as an indication of the need for spiritual detachment, but such an uncompromising suppression of all outward tokens of affection is not typical of the *Sayings of the Desert Fathers*, still less of Varsanuphius and John.

A third gift of the spiritual father is *the power to transform the human environment*, both the material and the non-material. The gift of healing, possessed by so many of the startsi, is one aspect of this power. More generally, the starets helps his disciples to perceive the world as God created it and as God desires it once more to be. "Can you take too much joy in your Father's works?" asks Thomas Traherne. "He is Himself in everything." The true starets is one who discerns this universal presence of the Creator throughout creation, and assissts others to discern it. In the words of William Blake, "If the doors of perception were cleansed, everything will appear to man as it is, infinite." For the man who dwells in God, there is nothing mean and trivial: he sees everything in the light of Mount Tabor. "What is a merciful heart?" inquires St. Isaac the Syrian. "It is a heart that burns with love for the whole of creation — for men, for the birds, for the beasts, for the demons, for every creature. When a man with such a heart as this thinks of the creatures or looks at them, his eyes are filled with tears. An overwhelming compassion makes his heart grow small and weak, and he cannot endure to hear or see any suffering, even the smallest pain, inflicted upon any creature. Therefore he never ceases to pray, with tears even for the irrational animals, for the enemies of truth, and for those who do him evil, asking that they may be guarded and receive God's mercy. And for the reptiles also he prays with a great compassion, which rises up endlessly in his heart until he shines again and is glorious like God."[19]

An all embracing love, like that of Dostoevsky's starets Zosima, transfigures its object, making the human environment transparent, so that the uncreated energies of God shine through it. A momentary glimpse of what this transfiguration involves is provided by the celebrated "conversation" between St. Seraphim of Sarov and Nicholas Motovilov, his spiritual child. They were walking in the forest one winter's day and St. Seraphim spoke of the need to acquire the Holy Spirit. This led Motovilov to ask how a man can know with certainty that he is "in the Spirit of God:"

> Then Fr. Seraphim took me very firmly by the shoulders and said: "My son, we are both at this moment in the Spirit of God. Why don't you look at me?"
>
> "I cannot look, Father," I replied, "because your eyes are flashing like lightning. Your face has become brighter than the sun, and it hurts my eyes to look at you."
>
> "Don't be afraid," he said. "At this very moment you have yourself become as bright as I am. You are yourself in the fullness of the Spirit of God at this moment; otherwise you would not be able to see me as you do ... but why, my son, do you not look me in the eyes? Just look, and don't be afraid; the Lord is with us."
>
> After these words I glanced at his face, and there came over me an even greater reverent awe. Imagine in the center of the sun, in the dazzling light of its mid-day rays, the face of a man talking to you. You see the movement of his lips and the changing expression of his eyes and you hear his voice, you feel someone holding your shoulders, yet you do not see his hands, you do not even see yourself or his body, but only a

blinding light spreading far around for several yards and lighting up with its brilliance the snow-blanket which covers the forest glade and the snowflakes which continue to fall unceasingly.[20]

Such are by God's grace, the gifts of the starets. But what of the spiritual child? How does he contribute to the mutual relationship between father and son in God?

Briefly, what he offers is his full and unquestioning obedience. As a classic example, there is the story in the *Sayings of the Desert Fathers* about the monk who was told to plant a dry stick in the sand and to water it daily. So distant was the spring from his cell that he had to leave in the evening to fetch the water and he only returned in the following morning. For three years he patiently fulfilled his Abba's command. At the end of this period, the stick suddenly put forth leaves and bore fruit. The Abba picked the fruit, took it to the church, and invited the monks to eat, saying, "Come and taste the fruit of obedience."[21]

Another example of obedience is the monk Mark who was summoned by his Abba, while copying a manuscript, and so immediate was his response that he did not even complete the circle of the letter O that he was writing. On another occasion, as they walked together, his Abba saw a small pig; testing Mark, he said, "Do you see that buffalo, my child?" "Yes, Father," replied Mark. "And you see how powerful its horns are?" "Yes, Father," he answered once more without demur.[22] Abba Joseph of Panepho, following a similar policy, tested the obedience of his disciples by assigning ridiculous tasks to them, and only if they complied would he then give them sensible commands.[23] Another geron instructed his disciple to steal things from the cells of the brethren;[24] yet another told his disciple (who had not been entirely truthful with him) to throw his son into the furnace.[25]

Such stories are likely to make a somewhat ambivalent impression on the modern reader. They seem to reduce the disciple to an infantile or sub-human level, depriving him of all power of judgment and moral choice. With indignation we ask: "Is this the 'glorious liberty of the children of God'?" (Rom. 8:21)

Three points must here be made. In the first place, the obedience offered by the spiritual son to his Abba is not forced but willing and voluntary. It is the task of the starets to take up our will into his will, but he can only do this if by our own free choice we place it in his hands. He does not break our will, but accepts it from us as a gift. A submission that is forced and involuntary is obviously devoid of moral value; the staret asks of each one that he offer to God his heart, not his external actions.

The voluntary nature of obedience is vividly emphasized in the ceremony of the tonsure at the Orthodox rite of monastic profession. The scissors are placed upon the Book of the Gospels, and the novice must himself pick them up and give them to the abbot. The abbot immediately replaces them on the Book of the Gospels. Again the novice takes up the scissors, and again they are replaced. Only when the novice gives him the scissors for the third time does the abbot proceed to cut his hair. Never thereafter will the monk have the right to say to the abbot or the brethren: "My personality is constricted and suppressed here in the monastery; you have deprived me of my freedom." No one has taken away his freedom, for it was he himself who took up the scissors and placed them three times in the abbot's hand.

But this voluntary offering of our freedom is obviously something that cannot be made once and for all, by a single gesture. There must be a continual offering, extending over our whole life; our growth in Christ is measured precisely by the increasing degree of our self-giving. Our freedom must be offered anew each day and each hour, in constantly varying ways; and this means that the relation between starets and disciple is not static but dynamic, not unchanging but infinitely diverse. Each day and each hour, under the guidance of his Abba, the disciple will face new situations, calling for a different response, a new kind of self-giving.

In the second place, the relation between starets and spiritual child is not one- but two-sided. Just as the starets enables the disciples to see themselves as they truly are, so it is the disciples who reveal the starets to himself. In most instances, a man does not realize that he is called to be a starets until others come to him and insist on placing themselves under his guidance. This reciprocity continues throughout the relationship between the two. The spiritual father does not possess an exhaustive program, neatly worked out in advance and imposed in the same manner upon everyone. On the contrary, if he is a true starets, he will have a different word for each; and since the word which he gives is on the deepest level, not his own but the Holy Spirit's, he does not know in advance what that word will be. The starets proceeds on the basis, not of abstract rules but of concrete human situations. He and his disciple enter each situation together, neither of them knowing beforehand exactly what the outcome will be, but each waiting for the enlightenment of the Spirit. Each of them, the spiritual father as well as the disciple, must learn as he goes.

The mutuality of their relationship is indicated by certain stories in the *Sayings of the Desert Fathers*, where an unworthy Abba has a spiritual son far better than himself. The disciple, for example, detects his Abba in the sin of fornication, but pretends to have noticed nothing and remains under his charge; and so, through the patient humility of his new disciple, the spiritual father is brought eventually to repentance and a new life. In such a case, it is not the spiritual father who helps the disciple, but the reverse. Obviously such a situation is far from the norm, but it indicates that the disciple is called to give as well as to receive.

In reality, the relationship is not two-sided but triangular, for in addition to the starets and his disciple there is also a third partner, God. Our Lord insisted that we should call no man "father," for we have only one father, who is in Heaven (Matthew 13:8-10). The starets is not an infallible judge or a final court of appeal, but a fellow-servant of the living God; not a dictator, but a guide and companion on the way. The only true "spiritual director," in the fullest sense of the word, is the Holy Spirit.

This brings us to the third point. In the Eastern Orthodox tradition at its best, the spiritual father has always sought to avoid any kind of constraint and spiritual violence in his relations with his disciple. If, under the guidance of the Spirit, he speaks and acts with authority, it is with the authority of humble love. The words of starets Zosima in *The Brothers Karamazov* express an essential aspect of spiritual fatherhood: "At some ideas you stand perplexed, especially at the sight of men's sin, uncertain whether to combat it by force or by humble love. Always decide, 'I will combat it by humble love.' If you make up your mind about that once and for all, you can conquer the whole world. Loving humility is a terrible force; it is the strongest of all things and there is nothing like it."

Anxious to avoid all mechanical constraint, many spiritual fathers in the Christian East refused to provide their disciples with a rule of life, a set of external commands to be applied automatically. In the words of a contemporary Romanian monk, the starets is "not a legislator but a mystagogue."[26] He guides others, not by imposing rules, but by sharing his life with them. A monk told Abba Poemen, "Some brethren have come to live with me; do you want me to give them orders?" "No," said the Old Man. "But, Father," the monk persisted, "they themselves want me to give them orders." "No," repeated Poemen, "be an example to them but not a lawgiver."[27] The same moral emerges from the story of Isaac the Priest. As a young man, he remained first with Abba Kronios and then with Abba Theodore of Pherme; but neither of them told him

what to do. Isaac complained to the other monks and they came
and remonstrated with Theodore. "If he wishes," Theodore replied
eventually, "let him do what he sees me doing."[28] When Varsanuphius was asked to supply a detailed rule of life, he refused,
saying: "I do not want you to be under the law, but under grace."
And in other letters he wrote: "You know that we have never imposed chains upon anyone ... Do not force men's free will, but sow
in hope, for our Lord did not compel anyone, but He preached the
good news, and those who wished hearkened to Him."[29]

Do not force men's free will. The task of the spiritual father is not
to destroy a man's freedom, but to assist him to see the truth for
himself; not to suppress a man's personality, but to enable him to
discover himself, to grow to full maturity and to become what he
really is. If on occasion the spiritual father requires an implicit and
seemingly "blind" obedience from his disciple, this is never done as
an end in itself, nor with a view to enslaving him. The purpose of
this kind of "shock treatment" is simply to deliver the disciple from
his false and illusory "self," so that he may enter into true freedom.
The spiritual father does not impose his own ideas and devotions,
but he helps the disciple to find his own special vocation. In the
words of a 17th-century Benedictine, Dom Augustine Baker: "The
director is not to teach his own way, nor indeed any determinate
way of prayer, but to instruct his disciples how they may
themselves find out the way proper for them ... In a word, he is only
God's usher, and must lead souls in God's way, and not his own."[30]

In the last resort, what the spiritual father gives to his disciple is
not a code of written or oral regulations, not a set of techniques for
meditation, but a personal relationship. Within this personal relationship the Abba grows and changes as well as the disciple, for
God is constantly guiding them both. He may on occasion provide
his disciple with detailed verbal instructions, with precise answers
to specific questions. On other occasions he may fail to give any
answer at all, either because he does not think that the question
needs an answer, or because he himself does not yet know what the
answer should be. But these answers — or this failure to answer — are always given the framework of a personal relationship.
Many things cannot be said in words, but can be conveyed through
a direct personal encounter.

And what is one to do, if he cannot find a spiritual father?

He may turn, in the first place, to *books*. Writing in 15th-century
Russia, St. Nil Sorsky laments the extreme scarcity of qualified
spiritual directors; yet how much more frequent they must have
been in his day than in ours! Search diligently, he urges, for a sure

and trustworthy guide. "However, if such a teacher cannot be found, then the Holy Fathers order us to turn to the Scriptures and listen to Our Lord Himself speaking."[31] Since the testimony of Scripture should not be isolated from the continuing witness of the Spirit in the life of the Church, the inquirer will also read the works of the Fathers, and above all the Philokalia. But there is an evident danger here. The starets adapts his guidance to the inward state of each; books offer the same advice to everyone. How is the beginner to discern whether or not a particular text is applicable to his own situation? Even if he cannot find a spiritual father in the full sense, he should at least try to find someone more experienced than himself, able to guide him in his reading.

It is possible to learn also from visiting places where divine grace has been exceptionally manifested and where prayer has been especially concentrated. Before taking a major decision, and in the absence of other guidance, many Orthodox Christians will go on pilgrimage to Jerusalem or Mount Athos, to some monastery or the tomb of a saint, where they will pray for enlightenment. This is the way in which I have reached the more difficult decisions in my life.

Thirdly, we can learn from *religious communities* with an established tradition of the spiritual life. In the absence of a personal teacher, the monastic environment can serve as guru; we can receive our formation from the ordered sequence of the daily program, with its periods of liturgical and silent prayer, with its balance of manual labor, study, and recreation.[32] This seems to have been the chief way in which St. Seraphim of Sarov gained his spiritual training. A well-organized monastery embodies, in an accessible and living form, the inherited wisdom of many starets. Not only monks, but those who come as visitors for a longer or shorter period, can be formed and guided by the experience of community life.

It is indeed no coincidence that the kind of spiritual fatherhood that we have been describing emerged initially in 4th century Egypt, not within the fully organized communities under St. Pachomius, but among the hermits and in the semi-eremitic milieu of Nitria and Scetis. In the former, spiritual direction was provided by Pachomius himself, by the superiors of each monastery, and by the heads of individual "houses" within the monastery. The Rule of St. Benedict also envisages the abbot as spiritual father, and there is no provision for further development of a more "charismatic" type. In time, of course, the coenobitic communities incorporated many of the traditions of spiritual fatherhood as developed among the hermits, but the need for those traditions has always been less intensely felt in the coenobia, precisely because direction is provided by the corporate life pursued under the guidance of the Rule.

Finally, before we leave the subject of the absence of the starets, it is important to recognize the extreme flexibility in the relationship between starets and disciple. Some may see their spiritual father daily or even hourly, praying, eating, and working with him, perhaps sharing the same cell, as often happened in the Egyptian Desert. Others may see him only once a month or once a year; others, again, may visit a starets on but a single occasion in their entire life, yet this will be sufficient to set them on the right path. There are, furthermore, many different types of spiritual father; few will be wonder-workers like St. Seraphim of Sarov. There are numerous priests and laymen who, while lacking the more spectacular endowments of the startsi, are certainly able to provide others with the guidance that they require.

Many people imagine that they cannot find a spiritual father, because they expect him to be of a particular type: they want a St. Seraphim, and so they close their eyes to the guides whom God is actually sending to them. Often their supposed problems are not so very complicated, and in reality they already know in their own heart what the answer is. But they do not like the answer, because it involves patient and sustained effort on their part: and so they look for a deus ex machina who, by a single miraculous word, will suddenly make everything easy. Such people need to be helped to an understanding of the true nature of spiritual direction.

In conclusion, I wish briefly to recall two startsi of our own day, whom I have had the happiness of knowing personally. The first is Father Amphilochios (†1970), abbot of the Monastery of St. John on the Island of Patmos, and spiritual father to a community of nuns which he had founded not far from the Monastery. What most distinguished his character was his gentleness, the warmth of his affection, and his sense of tranquil yet triumphant joy. Life in Christ, as he understood it, is not a heavy yoke, a burden to be carried with resignation, but a personal relationship to be pursued with eagerness of heart. He was firmly opposed to all spiritual violence and cruelty. It was typical that, as he lay dying and took leave of the nuns under his care, he should urge the abbess not to be too severe on them: "They have left everything to come here, they must not be unhappy."[33] When I was to return from Patmos to England as a newly-ordained priest, he insisted that there was no need to be afraid of anything.

My second example is Archbishop John (Maximovich), Russian bishop in Shanghai, in Western Europe, and finally in San Francisco († 1966). Little more than a dwarf in height, with tangled hair and beard, and with an impediment in his speech, he possessed more than a touch of the "Fool in Christ." From the time of his profession as a monk, he did not lie down on a bed to sleep at night; he went on working and praying, snatching his sleep at odd moments in the 24 hours. He wandered barefoot through the streets of Paris, and once he celebrated a memorial service among the tram lines close to the port of Marseilles. Punctuality had little meaning for him. Baffled by his unpredictable behavior, the more conventional among his flock sometimes judged him to be unsuited for the administrative work of a bishop. But with his total disregard of normal formalities he succeeded where others, relying on worldy influence and expertise, had failed entirely — as when, against all hope and in the teeth of the "quota" systems, he secured the admission of thousands of homeless Russian refugees to the U.S.A.

In private conversation he was very gentle, and he quickly won the confidence of small children. Particularly striking was the intensity of his intercessory prayer. When possible, he liked to celebrate the Divine Liturgy daily, and the service often took twice or three times the normal space of time, such was the multitude of those whom he commemorated individually by name. As he prayed for them, they were never mere names on a lengthy list, but always persons. One story that I was told is typical. It was his custom each year to visit Holy Trinity Monastery at Jordanville, N.Y. As he left, after one such visit, a monk gave him a slip of paper with four names of those who were gravely ill. Archbishop John received thousands upon thousands of such requests for prayer in the course of each year. On his return to the monastery some twelve months later, at once he beckoned to the monk, and much to the latter's surprise, from the depths of his cassock Archbishop John produced the identical slip of paper, now crumpled and tattered. "I have been praying for your friends," he said, "but two of them" — he pointed to their names — "are now dead and the other two have recovered." And so indeed it was.

Even at a distance he shared in the concerns of his spiritual children. One of them, superior of a small Orthodox monastery in Holland, was sitting one night in his room, unable to sleep from anxiety over the problems which faced him. About three o'clock in the morning, the telephone rang; it was Archbishop John, speaking from several hundred miles away. He had rung to say that it was time for the monk to go to bed.

Such is the role of the spiritual father. As Varsanuphius expressed it, "I care for you more than you care for yourself."

Kallistos Ware

Footnotes:

1. On spiritual fatherhood in the Christian East, see the well-documented study by I. Hausherr, S. L., *Direction Spirituelle en Orient d'Autrefois* (Orientalia Christiana analecta, 144: Rome 1955). An excellent portrait of a great starets in 19th-century Russia is provided by J. B. Dunlop, *Staretz Amvrosy: Model for Dostoevsky's Staretz Zossima* (Belmont, Mass. 1972): compare also I. de Beausobre, *Macarius, Starets of Optina: Russian Letters of Direction 1834-1860* (London, 1944). For the life and writings of a Russian starets in the present century, see Archimandrite Sofrony, *The Undistorted Image. Staretz Silouain: 1866-1938* (London, 1858)

2. *Apophthegmata Patrum*, alphabetical collection (Migne, *P.G.*, 65, pp. 37-8).

3. *Les Apophtegemes des Pères du Désert*, by J. C. Guy, S.jj. (Texltes de Spiritualité Orientale, No. 1: Etiolles, 1968), pp. 112, 158.

4. A. Elchaninov, *The Diary of a Russian Priest*, (London, 1967, p. 54)

5. I use "charismatic" in the restricted sense customarily given to it by contemporary writers. But if that word indicates one who has received the gifts or charismata of the Holy Spirit, then the ministerial priest, ordained through the episcopal laying on of hands, is as genuinely a "charismatic" as one who speaks with tongues.

6. *The Life of St. Antony*, chapters 87 and 81 (P.G. 26, 965A, and 957A.)

7. Quoted in Igumen Chariton, *The Art of Prayer: An Orthodox Anthology* (London, 1966), p. 164.

8. *Apophthegmata Patrum*, alphabetical collection, Theophilus the Archbishop, p. 2. In the Christian East, the Patriarch of Alexandria bears the title "Pope."

9. *Ibid.*, Antony, p. 27.

10. *Ibid.*, Antony, p. 24.

11. Compare Ignaty's contemporary, Bishop Theophan the Recluse († 1894) and St. Tikhon of Zadonsk († 1753).

12. Three of the great banes of the 20th century are shorthand, duplicators and photocopying machines. If chairmen of committees and those in seats of authority were forced to write out personally in longhand everything they wanted to communicate to others, no doubt they would choose their words with greater care.

13. Evergetinos, *Synagoge*, I, 20 (ed. Victor Matthaiou, I, Athens, 1957, pp. 168-9).

14. *Apophthegmata Patrum*, alphabetical collection, Poemen, p. 8.

15. For the importance of a spiritual father's prayers, see for example *Les Apophtegmes des Pères du Désert*, tr. Guy, "série des dits anonymes", p. 160.

Modern Spirituality

Footnotes: cont.

16. *The Book Varsanuphius and John*, edited by Sotirios Schoinas (Volos, 1960), pp. 208, 39, 353, 110 and 23g.
A critical edition of part of the Greek text, accompanied by an English translation, has been prepared by D. J. Chitty: *Varsanuphius and John, Questions and Answers*, (Patrologia Orientalis, XXXI, 3, Paris, 1966).

17. *Apophthegmata Patrum*, alphabetical collection, Antony, p. 16.

18. *Ibid.*, John the Theban, p. 1.

19. *Mystic Treatises of Isaac of Nineveh*, tr. by A. J. Wensinck, (Amsterdam, 1923), p. 341.

20. "Conversation of St. Seraphim on the Aim of the Christian Life," in *A Wonderful Revelation to the World* (Jordanville, N.Y., 1953), pp. 23-24.

21. *Apophthegmata Patrum*, alphabetical collection, John Colobos, p. 1.

22. *Ibid.*, Mark the Disciple of Silvanus, pp. 1, 2.

23. *Ibid.*, Joseph of Panepho, p. 5.

24. *Ibid.*, Saio, p. 1. The geron subsequently returned the things to their rightful owners.

25. *Les Apophtegmes des Pères du Désert*, tr. Guy, "série des dits anonymes," p. 162. There is a parallel story in the alphabetical collection Sisoes, p. 10; cf. Abraham and isaac (Gen. 22).

26. Fr. André Scrima, "La Tradition du Père Spirituel dans l'Eglise D'Orient." *Hermés*. 1967, No. 4, p. 83.

27. *Apophthegmata Patrum*, alphabetical collection, Poemen, p. 174.

28. *Ibid.*, Isaac the Priest, p 2.

29. *The Book of Varsamuphius and John*, pp. 23, 51, 35.

30. Quoted by Thomas Merton, *Spiritual Direction and Meditation*, (1960), p. 12.

31. "The Monastic Rule," in G. P. Fedotov, *A Treasury of Russian Spirituality*, (London, 1950) p. 96.

32. But see Thomas Merton, *op. cit.*, pp. 14-16, on the dangers of rigid monastic discipline without proper spiritual direction.

33. See. I. Gorainoff, "Holy Men of Patmos", *Sobornost* (The Journal of the Fellowship of St. Alban and St. Sergius), Series 6, No. 6 (1972) pp. 341-4.

The Beatitudes

Simon Tugwell

Simon Tugwell is a member of the Dominican order and is currently Regent of Studies for Blackfriars, the Dominican House of Studies at Oxford. He is the author of Prayer: Living with God, Prayer in Practice, The Way of the Preacher, Ways of Imperfection, *and* The Beatitudes, *from which the following selection was taken.*

There is no doubt that the beatitudes have played a quite special role in Christian thinking about life. Bossuet places them at the beginning of the meditations which he put together for the use of his Visitation nuns, saying, "If the sermon on the mount is the précis of all Christian doctrine, the eight beatitudes are the précis of the whole of the sermon on the mount."[1] St. Dominic is said to have prayed especially for the gifts of the Holy spirit to be given to the Order he had founded "so that both he and his brethren might find it their joy and delight to live in the spirit of the beatitudes."[2] The connexion between the beatitudes and the gifts of the Holy Spirit was made first by St. Augustine, who also worked in the seven petitions of the Lord's Prayer.[3] Medieval theologians who preferred a more stratified view of life declared that the beatitudes outline a perfection even higher than promised by the gifts of the Spirit.[4] The compilers of the present lectionary of the Roman Church could find no text more appropriate than this for the Feast of All Saints.

Nevertheless, the beatitudes make a puzzling text. And the more one thinks about them, the more puzzling they become. On the one hand, they obviously call us to a tremendous height of spiritual and ethical achievement, to a righteousness which goes even further than that of the scribes and Pharisees (such as the Lord requires of his disciples — Matt. 5:20); yet, at the same time, they seem almost to canonize qualities which are the very antithesis of all achievement and success.

This is, of course, a paradox which we find elsewhere in the New Testament. Christian maturity is not just a matter of pulling ourselves together and being very impressive characters who have got it all right, who know exactly what it means to be a Christian and who have the will-power and the staying power actually to live up to it.

St. Paul might seem to be a decidedly strong-willed person; yet he wrestled and wrestled in vain with his mysterious "thorn in the flesh." When he pleaded to be rid of it, the Lord only answered him, "My grace is enough." St. Paul had to learn that it is precisely in weakness that strength is made perfect (2 Cor. 12:7-9). Our strength is the strength of God, but the strength of God given to man and so revealed curiously in weakness.

And it was surely from the experience of this that St. Paul learned to talk even about the weakness of God (1 Cor. 1:25). God does not come into our world with the toughness of an omnipotent thug, to sort everything and everybody out. He himself has chosen the way of weakness. There is something about God which is better expressed in weakness than in strength, in foolishness than in wisdom, in poverty than in richness. The story of the earthly life of Jesus Christ is a story of human failure, of human poverty, of human foolishness. And yet that is the revelation of God in human terms. And we who are followers of Jesus Christ are called to be imitators of him, and so should not be at all surprised to find that one of the arts we have to learn is the sublime art of weakness.

That certainly does not mean that we should simply be complacent in our weakness and think that there is no room for effort. There is plenty of evidence in the writings of the saints and in the bible that there is a very real place for effort. But effort can be misplaced.

St. Paul, on the basis of his own experience as a Pharisee and as a Christian, gives us an important statement of the nature of Christian perfection. He claims that, as a Pharisee, he had achieved the kind of righteousness enshrined in the Jewish law, as understood by the Pharisees: he was, he says, "blameless according to the righteousness which is in the law" (Phil. 3:6). But, as a Christian, he has no further use for that kind of righteousness, for that kind of accomplishment.

It is all too easy for us to treat the Pharisees as embodying all that is worst in humankind. But in fact they were probably the best men of their time, the most religious, the most devoted to the will of God, the most eager to express their loyalty to him in obedience to his every word, the most determined never to compromise with the world around them. But, as St. Paul came to see it in retrospect, they were exposed to a fatal flaw: the trouble with their outstanding righteousness was that, all too easily, it could be viewed precisely as *their* righteousness. It was a righteousness that could be measured, so that, at a certain point, you could say that you had now achieved it. This meant that it could all too easily come adrift from its original inspiration in devotion to God and become self-sufficient, an end in itself.

But how tempting it is to define righteousness in such a way that we can, at least conceivably, one day declare ourselves to have arrived at it. How lovely it would be to be able to go striding boldly into church, like the Pharisee in the Lord's parable, and say, "I thank you, God, I am doing splendidly" (cf. Luke 18.10ff). How humble we should be, how ready to acknowledge that it was all due to God's grace — and yet how insufferably conceited, and how abysmally dull.

The requirements of the Lutheran polemic have, to some extent, obscured the real objection that is being brought against the Pharisees. it is not that they are laying claim to some righteousness that they have achieved *on their own*, in opposition to a righteousness conceded by the grace of God. There is no suggestion in the Lord's parable that the Pharisee is being hypocritical in thanking God for his own happy condition. So far as we can tell, the Pharisees were probably quite prepared to acknowledge their dependence on God's grace; there are some early Rabbinic texts which express such dependence in the most emphatic terms.[5] Of course there is the risk that human beings will forget their dependence on God, and this is a part of St. Paul's complaint; but the far more essential criticism is that the Pharisaic concept of righteousness is such that it allows a man to be self-consciously righteous, to contemplate himself in his righteousness, to treat it as something he can possess as his own, whether or not he also thinks that he has achieved it on his own.

The basic form of complacency, after all, is that a person is pleased with himself. Someone may quite easily be complacent about his or her gifts, even while acknowledging that they are gifts. We can be self-satisfied about our good looks or our intelligence without having to suppose that we have created them ourselves. It is only a subdivision of complacency to be smug because we take full credit for ourselves to ourselves.

And complacency can enter even into our humility. Even when we go to confession, we can, more or less surreptitiously, be concerned with our own image of ourselves.

In Graham Greene's novel, *The Power and the Glory*, the whiskey priest on one occasion interrupts an old woman penitent who is prattling on and tells her:

"Remember your real sins." "But I'm a good woman, father," she squeaked at him with astonishment. "Then what are you doing here, keeping away the bad people?" He said, "Have you any love for anyone but yourself?" "I love God, father," she said haughtily. He took a quick look at her in the light of the candle burning on the floor — the hard old raisin eyes under the black shawl — another of the pious — like himself. "How do you know? Loving God isn't any different from loving a man — or a child. It's wanting to be with Him, to be near Him." He made a hopeless gesture with his hands. "It's wanting to protect Him from yourself."[6]

If all else fails, we can even get a certain smug joy out of watching our own honesty, our own self-exposure, our own humiliation.

The point was raised formally in a medieval controversy about the essential content of heavenly bliss. Durandus of St. Pourçain, a Dominican noted for his opposition to orthodox Thomism, maintained that what the blessed enjoy immediately and directly is not God, but their own vision of God. He suggests a comparison with a man's love of wine: it is not the wine, as such, that satisfies him, but his drinking of the wine.[7]

This view is very firmly refused by Meister Eckhart, who is followed and, indeed, quoted on the matter by Bl. Henry Suso.[8] The reflex movement of self-consciousness would be a distraction from the beatitude of simply knowing God. According to the text in St. John (17:3), eternal life is in knowing God, not in knowing that we know God. It is not that we are unconscious of our own knowledge of God or of our bliss; but the consciousness of ourselves is not the actual object of our bliss, it is not that that actually makes us happy.

Discussion of what heaven is like is, perhaps, never going to obtain for us all that much clarity about eternal life, because we cannot really conceive of it so long as we are still bound by the conditions of life in this world. Maybe in that *tota simul possessio*[9] in which all the particular kinds of enjoyment which we now know only in separation from one another form only one complete enjoyment, some kind of self-consciousness which might be noxious as a distinct phenomenon in itself will be fully innocent and appropriate. But the usefulness of attempting to make projections about eternity is that they can help us to focus on the trends which are discernible in different kinds of approach to life on earth. Can we really envisage spending eternity gazing at our own contentment, saying to ourselves, "There! I made it!"? In its own way, that is just as absurd as Agatha Christie's character who cannot imagine heaven as being anything other than a continual occasion for her to make herself useful. The only picture of herself that she can really enjoy is the picture of herself as the devoted servant of her loved ones (who, of course, have either to evade or to endure with as much good grace as they can the unceasing persecution of her devoted service).[10]

The danger with our good works, our spiritual accomplishments, and all the rest of it, is that we shall construct out of them a picture of ourselves in which, effectively, we shall situate our happiness. Complacency in ourselves will then replace delight in God.

St. Paul's concept of Christian perfection is radically incompatible with this kind of complacency, because it forces our attention constantly away from ourselves and our achievements and obliges us to look ahead, to God in whom all goodness dwells. His goal is

> to gain Christ and to be found in him, not having any righteousness of my own from the law, but having the righteousness which exists through faith in Christ, the righteousness which comes from God and is built on faith.

He makes no claim, as yet, to have arrived at his goal; what he does is simply to forget what lies behind and stretch out to what lies ahead. And it is precisely this, he says, that is the proper attitude for those who "are perfect." Perfection means the continual striving ahead, not any conviction of achievement (Phil. 3:12-15).

This model of perfection is developed at length by St. Gregory of Nyssa, especially in his *Life of Moses*. The only definition of virtue, he says, is that it is undefined, unbounded.[11] Moses' ascent into the darkness on Mount Sinai is taken as a symbol of the ascent of the soul of man, constantly going beyond itself and beyond all kinds of imaginative or conceptual representation of God.[12] And this process never ends. At no point can we say, "That's it." St. Gregory even envisages eternity like this.[13] Maybe this is not an acceptable view of eternity, but it is a valuable projection because of the light it sheds on temporal life.

It is with a similar concern, surely, to disqualify complacency that our Lord tells us, when we have done everything we ought to have done, not to pat ourselves on the back, but to say, "We are useless servants" (Luke 17:10).

And this is at least part of the point of the saying that we must become like little children, if we want to enter the kingdom of God (Matt. 18:3). In all three synoptic gospels there is what is surely meant to be a significant contrast implicit in the juxtaposition of the scene with the little children and the story of the rich man who wants to know what he should do to inherit eternal life. The rich man seemingly has everything; not only has he got wealth, he is evidently a thoroughly good man, who has kept all the commandments since he was young. (It is only in Matthew that he is said to be still a young man.) The Lord loves him as soon as he sees him. But he sends him away with a flea in his ear, for all that, commenting, 'How hard it is for those with money to enter the kingdom of God." The disciples are dumbfounded. "Then who can be saved?" they ask. This rich man would seem to be the ideal candidate for eternal life. But maybe that is the whole point. The message that our Lord wishes to put across is precisely that, however well placed we are, it is still, quite strictly, *impossible* for us to enter the Kingdom of God. When the disciples ask who can be saved, the only answer they get is, "It is impossible with men, but not with God" (Mark 10:13ff etc.).

The rich man wanted to discover something he could *do* in order to inherit eternal life, he wanted to keep himself in the picture. But there is nothing that any of us can do. We must simply *receive* the kingdom of God like little children.[14] And little children are precisely those who have not done anything. The ancient world was not sentimental about children and had few illusions about any pretended innate goodness in them. The Lord is not suggesting that heaven is a great playground for Arcadian infants. The children are our model because they have no claim on heaven. If they are close to God, it is because they are incompetent, not because they are innocent. They contrast with the rich man simply because there is no question of their having yet been able to merit anything. If they receive anything, it can only be as a gift.

When our Lord tells us to become like little children, he is bidding us forget what lies behind. Children have no past. Whatever we have done in the past, be it good or evil, great or small, it is, strictly speaking, irrelevant to our stance before God. It is only *now* that we are in the presence of God. And "now," as de Caussade brings out, is always a "desert,"[15] in which we can have no sense of where we have got to. It is from our past and from our attempts to programme the future that we insert the present into some kind of picture of our lives and ourselves. But in the naked "now" there is no room for any picture of ourselves. And that is where God is. We may, if we like, prefer to call it "nowhere."[16]

"Look, I am making everything new," declares the risen Lord in the great vision of the Apocalypse (Apoc. 21:5). We cannot bring the luggage of our past with us into the new moment of God's making.

The past is, perhaps, not totally lost, but it is no longer ours; it is in the hands of God and is his business. It will be retrieved in the *tota simul possessio* of eternity, but should not be stored away on earth. As far as we are concerned, we must realize that we are like children, at the beginning, not the end, of a road. Whatever past achievements might bring us honour, whatever past disgraces might make us blush, all of these have been crucified with Christ; they exist no more except in the deep recesses of God's eternity, where good is enhanced into glory and evil miraculously established as part of the greater good.

As we grow older, we inevitably acquire an ever-increasing past. The danger is that we shall see ourselves and present ourselves too much in terms of that past. This is why we are generally so much concerned to have some kind of interpretation of our own past ready at least for our own use. Most of us probably spend quite a lot of time "editing" our autobiographies, so that we shall have the "official version" of the story ready for judgement day.

But does it really matter? Are we not just wasting our time? Do we have to justify or excuse or commend ourselves like this? Can we do it anyway? Is it all really not just designed to safeguard our complacent contemplation of our own picture of ourselves?

"Look, I am making everything new." The newness of God calls for and calls forth a corresponding newness in us. Our anxious totting up of our past shows a misconception of what it means for us to be confronted with God. This is why the stories of death-bed conversions are so important a part of Christian tradition; we are not, in the final analysis, our past, we are whatever we are in God's present.

We must not misinterpret this as signifying that we ought, in principle, to be able to verify empirically that we are new like children at every moment of our lives. It is a theological statement that we are making, not a psychological one. There is no reason to suppose that we shall *feel* new. There clearly can sometimes be miraculous interventions which do create an entirely new situation, so that a state of affairs which had seemed insoluble suddenly rights itself or turns into something else; but we should certainly not presume on such miracles happening. And that is not only because it is never safe to presume on miracles happening, but also because if we did set up this particular kind of miracle as normative, we should be in serious danger of falsifying an important point of doctrine. If we were led to believe that somehow we ought to *feel* new the whole time in our relationship with God, we should simply be re-establishing a new pattern of the kind of Pharisaism rejected by St. Paul; we should be defining the criteria for a successful response to God, and so would end up with exactly the same hazard of complacency, even if the particular criteria of success were slightly different (laws of psychological wholeness or spirituality rather than laws of Mishnah).

One of the consequences for most of us of growing older (and I am not referring to becoming old — the process begins before we can walk or talk) is that we develop a sense of how one thing leads to another; and that makes it possible for us to become calculating. "If I do this, then I shall be in a good position for getting or achieving that." What we have to realize, and it is a difficult point for us to grasp, is that there is no such thing as a "good position" in our dealings with God.

Meister Eckhart in particular keeps on reminding us that we must grasp God in *everything*.[17] Anyone who insists on approaching God in any particular way "gets the way, but lets go of God."[18] We must be completely detached about all circumstances, external and internal; we must even be detached about detachment.[19] The truly spiritual person does not even seek tranquillity (of whose importance Eckhart elsewhere speaks in emphatic terms[20]), because he is in no way hampered by lack of it.[21] So all possible answers we might give to the question, "What shall I do to inherit eternal life?" are declared irrelevant and counter-productive; we are given no encouragement at all to entertain our feeling that if only we did not get these headaches, if only we had nicer neighbours, if only we knew how to pray, if only we were more humble, everything would go swimmingly.

We do not have to work out how to get ourselves into a good position for having a relationship with God, we do not have to design ways of explaining our position to him, we do not have to create a pretty face for ourselves, we do not have to achieve any state of feeling or understanding. The newness inherent in any situation of encounter with God is brought by him, not by us, and the newness it calls for in us is not a newness of physical or psychological or intellectual experience, it is simply a newness of being given to him (and that, too, is not a matter of psychological or any other kind of experience in itself, though it may, of course, lead to or involve some kind of transformation of our experience of life).

So, to return to the paradox with which we started, the beatitudes do indeed draw for us a picture of a kind of spiritual perfection and ethical achievement, but it is a kind of perfection which will be, almost by definition, not self-conscious of itself as perfection or achievement. It is a kind of perfection which even seems to render useless the whole familiar distinction between success and failure, achievement and non-achievement, which is such an important instrument in our normal analysis of life.

But then, what should we expect? If God is to be the measure of our perfection, and we are bidden to be "perfect as your heavenly Father is perfect" (Matt. 5:48), how could we ever begin to evaluate our progress, let alone commend ourselves on our development?

The stretching of righteousness beyond that of the Pharisees must profoundly alter our very concept of what it means to be righteous and even more of what if feels like to be righteous. If it is open-ended towards God, towards divine perfection, then it is no longer possible to reduce it to what can be quantified. Of course, a quantifiable element remains: it is still right and proper for us to say that murder is a sin, and that therefore abstaining from murder is a good thing. But such things no longer add up to a definition of righteousness, not even a working definition. When we have done all that we ought to have done and refrained from all that we ought to have refrained from, we are still only useless servants. And if we have done all that we ought not to have done and failed to do all that we ought to have done, our position is equally or almost equally unclear. Though it took many centuries for the church to arrive at our present position in which it is shockingly easy for, say, a murderer to be in good standing in the church, this has surely been a healthy development. The easiness of confession for every class of sinner, whatever problems it may cause to the relatively squeamish tastes of most believers, is an important attestation of the nature of our relationship with God in Christ.

As abba Theodotus said, "Do not judge a fornicator if you are chaste, otherwise you will be transgressing the law too. For he who said, 'Do not fornicate,' also said, 'Do not judge.' "[22]

We are all, equally, privileged but unentitled beggars before the door of God's mercy.

Footnotes:

1. Bossuet, *M5ed. Év.*, I 1 (p. 65).
2. *Nine Ways*, 7 (T p. 102; ET p. 38).
3. *SDM* I 11, II 38.
4. Cf. O. Lottin, *Psychologie et morale aux XII^c et XIII^c siecles*, III (Louvain 1949), pp. 360, 376, 389, 404, etc.

Footnotes: cont.

5. Cf. H. L. Strack & P. Billerbeck, *Kommentar zum Neuen Testament aus Talmud und Midrasch*, II (Munich 1924), on Luke 18:11. Our evidence for the Pharisees is deplorably scant, but there seems no reason to suppose that later Jewish texts expressing a strong view of dependence on God for all human goodness, including moral goodness, do not represent the attitude of the Pharisees. Josephus, at least, appears to regard it as a difference between them and the Sadducees that the latter ascribe moral achievement simply to human free will, whereas the Pharisees regard it as deriving from God (*Bell Jud*, II 8, 14). Cf. Emil Schurer, *The History of the Jewish People in the Age of Jesus Christ*, revised ed. by Geza Vermes, Fergus Millar & Matthew Black, vol. ii (Edinburgh, 1979) pp. 392ff; E. P. Sanders, *Paul and Palestinian Judaism* (London 1977) pp. 224, 297. The most impressive relevant Rabbinic texts are in BT *Ber* 16b-17a. One element in the picture is the doctrine that the soul implanted in each one of us by God is aboriginally completely pure: BT *Nid* 30b; *Shab* 152b; MR Lev 18:1; Philo, *Quis rerum* 105ff. Cf Hermas 28 (= *Mand* III), 109 (= *Sim* IX 32). That the nature of man is essentially good, in spite of sin, is an important element in Greek Christian theology of grace: cf. Athanasius, *VA* 20 (PG 26:872-3); Gregory of Nyssa, *Virg* XII 2-3 (= J 297.24-302.4). Pelagius tried to express the same thought, *Dem* 2 (PL 30:16-17), but fell foul of Augustine, which is why the idea does not generally feature in later western thought on the subject. For the doctrine that God reinforces every good move we make: BT *Shab* 104a, *Yom* 39a. Many relevant texts can be found in *Forms of Prayer for Jewish Worship*, I pp. 212ff (published by The Reform Synagogues of Great Britain 1977).

6. Graham Greene, *The Power and the Glory*, III ch. 1, p. 173.

7. *In Sent* I d. 1 q.2, p. 14.

8. Eckhart, QMa V 116-7 (= QMi 146-7, C1Fab 156, C1Fon 153); Suso *Little Book of Truth*, V (T p. 346, ET p. 195).

9. Cf. Boethius, *Consolation of Philosophy*, V prose 6.

10. Mary Westmacott (= Agatha Christie), *Absent in the Spring*, ch. 5, p. 70.

11. *VM* I 5 (= J 3:12-14).

12. *VM* II 163-9 (= J 87-9).

13. *Cant* V (= J 158-60, PG 44:876).

14. Cf. Thérèse of Lisieux, *DE* 6.8.8. (T pp. 308-9, ET p. 89): in response to her sister's question what she understood by "remaining a little child before the good God," she said,

    It is recognizing one's nothingness (*son néant*), expecting everything from the good God, just as a little child expects

Footnotes: cont.

everything from its father; it is not getting anxious about anything, not trying to make one's fortune. Even with the poor, a child is always given what it needs; but as soon as it grows up, its father refuses to go on supporting it and says to it: "Now you must go and work, you can look after yourself." It is to avoid having that said to me that I have always refused to grow up, because I felt that I was quite incapable of earning my living (*gagner ma vie*), earning my eternal life in heaven. So I have remained always little, having nothing else to do except pick flowers, flowers of love and sacrifice, and to offer them to the good God to give him pleasure. Being little is also not attributing to oneself the virtues that one practises, as if one believed oneself capable of achieving something, but recognizing that the good God puts this treasure into the hands of his little child for it to make use of it whenever it needs to; but it is always the good God's treasure. Finally it is never being disheartened by one's faults, because children often fall, but they are too little to do themselves much harm.

15. *Ab* p. 34 (ET II 2 §4).

16. Cf. *Cloud of Unknowing* ch. 67.

17. Eckhart, QMa V 203-4 (= QMi 59-60, C/Fab 68-9, C1Fon 65); QMa II 473-4 (= QMi 265, PE I 259).

18. QMa I 91 (= QMi 180, W 117).

19. QMa V 23 (= QMi 111, C1Fab 119, C1Fon 116).

20. QMa III 16 (= QMi 367, PE I 120).

22. QMa V 206 (= QMi 61, C1Fab 70, C1Fon 66); QMa II 81-2 (= QMi 292, W 137).

22. *AP* Nau 11.

Easter

Karl Rahner, S.J.

Karl Rahner, perhaps the most important Roman Catholic theologian of our time, died in 1983. He wrote voluminously, his Theological Investigations *being his best known and most important work. His prose was often dense and difficult, but he was also capable of direct and pastoral prose, as the following meditation on the Easter mystery makes clear.*

To do justice to the mystery of Easter joy with the stale words of human speech is rather difficult. This is so not only because every mystery of the Gospel penetrates only with difficulty into the narrow confines of human life — thereby making it even harder for our words to grasp and contain and express these mysteries — but because the Easter-message is the most human tidings of christianity. That is why we find it the most difficult message to understand. For what is most true, most obvious, and most easy, is the most difficult to be, to do, and to believe. That is to say, modern man bases his life on the unexpressed, and therefore all the more self-evident, prejudice that anything "religious" is merely an affair of the most interior heart and of the loftiest spirit — something that we must bring about by ourselves, something, therefore, that involves the difficulties and unreality of the heart's thoughts and moods.

But Easter tells us that God has done something. God himself. And his action has not merely gently touched the heart of a man here and there, so that they tremble slightly from an ineffable and nameless someone. God has raised his Son from the dead. God has quickened the flesh. God has conquered death. He had done this — he has conquered — not merely in the realm of inwardness, in the realm of thought, but in the realm where we, the glory of the human mind notwithstanding, are most really ourselves: in the actuality of this world, far from all "mere" thoughts and "mere" sentiments. He has conquered in the realm where we experience practically what we are in essence: children of the earth, who die.

Children of the earth — that is what we are. Our existence is caught up in birth and death, in the body and in the earth, in bread and in wine. The earth, in short, is our home. Of course the fine, delicate, perceiving mind that looks to the eternal, and the soul that gives life to everything, these two must be blended into this earthliness like a mysterious "essence of spirit" if it is to be all worthwhile and authentic. But the mind and the soul must be in the realm where we exist: on earth and in the body. They must be there as the eternal splendor of earthly beings. They cannot be there simply in the sense of a pilgrim who, like a misunderstood foreigner, roams phantom-like over the stage of the world in one short episode. We are children of the earth; we are too much a part of the earth to wish to take our leave from her once and for all.

It is true enough that for the earth to be bearable, heaven itself must be bestowed on us. Yet heaven must bow down and stand over this abiding earth as a blessed light; heaven must break forth in splendor from the dark womb of the earth.

We belong to this earth. But if it is impossible for us to be disloyal to the earth — not from any self-will or self-mastery, which does not befit the sons of the humble-earnest mother earth, but because we must be what we are — then we are mortally sick with a mysterious illness that sticks fast in the innermost part of our earthly being. Our great mother, the earth, is herself afflicted. She groans under the burden of transitoriness. Her happiest feast is suddenly like the beginning of a funeral. And when we hear her laugh, we tremble with fear lest in the next moment she weep beneath her laughter. She bears children who die; they are too weak to live forever, and yet they have too much spirit to relinquish eternal joy without a fight, because, unlike the beasts of the earth, they see the end before it is upon them, and they are not compassionately spared the fully conscious experience of that end. The earth bears children of infinite hearts, and, alas, what she gives them is too beautiful for them to scorn, and too poor to satisfy them fully, for they are insatiable.

Earth is the region of this unfortunate gap between the grand promise that does not set free and the scanty gift that does not liberate. And that is why she also becomes the rich plentiful soil of sin, as her children try to tear away from her more than she can rightly give. She may cry out that she herself was rent asunder in just this way by the original sin of the first man of the earth, whom we call Adam. But this changes nothing. Right now she is that hapless mother: too keenly alive and too beautiful to be able to send her children away from her so that they might win for themselves in a different world a new homeland, a homeland of eternal life; too poor to give them the fulfillment of that yearning which she gives them. And she brings forth both life and death, not one without the other, because she is always both, and never one nor the other. And we call this muddy mixture of life and death, of joy and sorrow, of creative activity and tedious duties — we call this our everyday life.

Here we are on the earth, our homeland forever; and yet, this does not suffice. This adventure to escape from what is earthly does not spring from cowardice, but from loyalty to our own nature. What are we to do? Listen to the good news of the resurrection of the Lord! Is Christ the Lord risen form the dead, or not? We believe in his resurrection, and therefore we confess that he died, that he descended into the kingdom of the dead, and that he rose on the third day. But what is the significance of all this and why is it a blessing for the children of the earth?

The incarnate Son of the Father has died; he who is the eternal fullness of divinity, the necessary, the boundless, the holy One, who is the Word of the Father even before time exists, and who is at the same time the child of this earth, the Son of the blessed Mother — this One has died. This is therefore the death of one who is at one and the same time the Son of God's fullness and the child of earth's indigence. But death does not mean — as we myopically suppose like the quite un-christian spiritualists — that his mind and his soul, the vessel of his eternal divinity, have wrenched themselves away from the world and the earth, and flown to God's vast splendor beyond the world. Death does not mean that his soul has escaped, simply because the body, which held it down to the earth, is broken in death, and because the murderous earth has shown that the child of everlasting light could find no homeland in her darkness.

"Was crucified, died, and was buried," we say, and to that we immediately add, "he descended into the lower regions and he rose from the dead." With this addition, "died" takes on a meaning entirely different from the notion of escaping from the world, the sense we are accustomed to give to death. Jesus himself said that he would descend into the heart of the world (Mt 12:40), into the heart of all earthly things where everything is linked together and is one, where death and futility hold sway in the midst of this consolidation. Down into death he has penetrated. He let himself be conquered by death — holy stratagem of eternal life — so that death would gulp him down into the innermost depths of the world. In this way, having descended to the very womb of the earth, to the radical unity of the world, he could give the earth his divine life forever.

Because he died, he belongs all the more to the earth. For when the body of a man is embedded in its grave of earth, the man (his soul, we say), even though in God's immediate presence after death, enters all the more into definitive unity with that one mysterious basis in which all spatial and temporal things are linked together, and the soul lives on, as from its root. By this death the Lord has descended into this lowest depth. Now he is there; futility and death are there no longer. In death he has become the heart of this earthly world, the divine heart in the innermost heart of the world. And here the earth, "behind" her continual development in space and time, sinks her root into the power of the all-mighty God.

Christ has risen from this one heart of all earthly things where realized unity and nothingness were no longer distinguishable. He has not risen for the purpose of departing once and for all from that heart of the world. He has not risen so that the travail of death which brings him forth anew might so bestow upon him God's life and light that he would leave behind him the dark womb of the earth, hopelessly barren. He has risen in his *body*. And this means that he has already begun to transform the world into himself. He has forever taken the world to himself; he is born anew as a child of this earth. But it is now an earth that is transfigured, an earth that is set free, that is untwisted, an earth that is established forever in him and that is forever redeemed from death and from futility. He rose, not to show that he had forsaken the grave of the earth, but to prove that he has definitively transformed even this grave of death — body and earth — into the glorious, immeasurable dwelling of the living God and of the God-filled soul of the Son.

The risen Lord has not moved out from earth's little hut. For, as a matter of fact, he still has his body — in a definitive and glorified state,yes, but still his body. It is a part of this earth that belongs to the earth forever as a share of her reality and her destiny. He has risen in order to reveal that through his death the life of freedom and of bliss remains forever rooted in the earth's narrow confines and in her grief, in the very center of her heart.

What we call his resurrection — and unthinkingly take to be his own private destiny — is only the first surface indication that all reality, behind what we usually call experience (which we consider so important), has already changed in the really decisive depth of things. His resurrection is like the first eruption of a volcano which shows that God's fire already burns in the innermost depths of the earth, and that everything shall be brought to a holy glow in his light. He rose to show that this has already begun. The new creation has already started, the new power of a transfigured earth is already being formed from the world's innermost heart, into which Christ descended by dying. Futility, sin and death are already conquered in the innermost realm of all reality, and only the "little while" (which we call history "A.D.") is needed until what has actually already happened appears everywhere in glory, and not only in the body of Jesus.

Because he did not begin to heal, to save, and to transfigure the world by transfiguring the symptoms on the surface, but began rather at the innermost root, we suppose that nothing has happened to the essence beneath this superficial area. Because the waters of grief and guilt still flow on the surface where we stand, we fancy that their source in the depths is not yet dried up. Because evil still carves new marks in the face of the earth, we conclude that in the deepest heart of reality love is dead. But these are only appearances, which we take for the reality of life.

Christ is risen because in death he conquered, and redeemed forever, the innermost center of all earthly existence. And, having risen, he has kept this innermost center in his control, and he continues to preserve it. If we acknowledge that he has gone away to God's heaven, this is only another way of saying that he withdraws from us for a while the tangibility of his tranfigured humanity. But this is only another way of saying that there is no longer any abyss between God and the world.

Christ is already in the midst of the poor things of this earth — the earth which we cannot leave because she is our mother. He is in the ineffable yearning of all creatures who, without knowing it, yearn for a share in the transfiguration of his body. He is in the history of the earth, whose blind course, with all its victories and all its crashing defeats, steers with uncanny precision towards the day when his splendor, transforming everything, will erupt out of the earth's own depths. He is in all the tears as hidden joy, and in every death as the life that conquers by seeming to die. He is in the beggar, to whom we give a coin, as the secret rich reward that returns to the giver. He is in the miserable defeats of his servants as the victory that belongs to God alone. He is in our weakness as the strength that dares to let itself seem weak, because it is invincible. He himself is even right in the midst of sin as the mercy of everlasting life that is prepared to be patient to the end. He is present as the mysterious law that triumphs and succeeds even when all order seems to be crumbling. He is with us like the light and air of day, which we do not notice; like the mysterious law of a motion that we do not grasp, because the segment of this motion that we ourselves experience is too short for a formula to be educed by us. But he is there. He is the heart of this earthly world and the mysterious seal of its eternal validity.

That is why we children of the earth may love the earth; that is why we must love her, even when she terrifies us and makes us tremble with her misery and her destiny of death. For ever since Christ, through his death and resurrection, penetrated the earth for all time, her misery has become provisional and a mere test of our faith in her innermost mystery, which is the risen One himself. Our experience does not tell us that he is the mysterious meaning of her misery; by no means! It is our faith that tells us this. The faith that offers blessed consolation to all that we experience in life, the faith that can love the earth because she is, or is in the process of becoming, the "body" of the risen One. We do not need to leave her, for the life of God dwells in her. When we want both the God of infinity (how can we help wanting him?) and the familiar earth, as it is and as it shall become, when we want both for our eternally free homeland, there is *one* path to *both!* For in the resurrection of the Lord, God has shown that he has accepted the earth for all time. *Caro cardo salutis,* said one of the Fathers of the Church in an untranslatable play on words: the flesh is the hinge of salvation.

The hereafter to every exigency of sin and of death is not somewhere in the life hereafter; it has come down to us and lives in the innermost reality of our flesh. The most sublime religiosity of seclusion from the world would not fetch the God of our life and the salvation of this earth from the distance of his eternity; and it would not even reach him in his. But he himself has come to us. And he has transformed what we are and what we still want to consider as the gloomy, earthly dwelling place of our "spiritual nature:" he has transformed *the flesh.* Ever since that event, mother earth bears nothing but transformed children. For his resurrection is the beginning of the resurrection of all flesh.

One thing, of course, is necessary for his event — which we can never undo — to become the blessedness of our existence: he must burst forth from the grave of our hearts. He must rise from the core of our being, where he is as power and promise. He is there, and yet something remains to be done. He is there, and yet it is still Holy Saturday, and it will continue to be Holy Saturday until the last day, until that day that will be the cosmic Easter. And this rising takes place beneath the freedom of our faith. It is taking place as an event of living faith that draws us into the colossal eruption of all earthly reality into its own glorification, the splendid tranfiguration that has already begun with the resurrection of Christ.

On the Invocation of the Name of Jesus

Lev Gillet

Lev Gillet, who died in 1980, was an Orthodox monk whose Roman Catholic background and frequent ecumenical contacts made him sympathetic to the richness of every Christian spiritual tradition. Under a name "A Monk of the Eastern Church" as well as his own name he wrote a number of books, among them Orthodox Spirituality, The Year of Grace of the Lord, In Thy Presence, *and* The Burning Bush. *The following selection from* On the Invocation of the Name of Jesus *describes an Orthodox spiritual practice which is increasingly used by Western Christians — the "Jesus Prayer" or "Prayer of the Heart."*

I. The Shape of the Invocation of the Name

And Jacob asked him and said: Tell me, I pray thee, thy name. And he said: Wherefore is it that thou dost ask after my name? And he blessed him there.

Genesis 32:29.

1. The invocation of the Name of Jesus can be put into many frames. It is for each person to find the form which is the most appropriate to his or her own prayer. But, whatever formula may be used, the heart and centre of the invocation must be the Holy Name itself, the word *Jesus*. There resides the whole strength of the invocation.

2. The Name of Jesus may either be used alone or be inserted in a more or less developed phrase. In the East the commonest form is: "Lord Jesus Christ, Son of God, have mercy upon me, a sinner."

One might simply say: "Jesus Christ," or "Lord Jesus." The invocation may even be reduced to one single word, "Jesus."

3. This last form — the Name of Jesus only — is the most ancient mould of the invocation of the Name. It is the shortest, the simplest and, as we think, the easiest. Therefore, without deprecating the other formulas, we suggest that the word "Jesus" alone should be used.

4. Thus, when we speak of the invocation of the Name, we mean the devout and frequent repetition of the Name itself, of the word "Jesus" without additions. The Holy Name is the prayer.

5. The Name of Jesus may be either pronounced or silently thought. In both cases there is a real invocation of the Name, verbal in the first case, and purely mental in the second. This prayer affords an easy transition from verbal to mental prayer. Even the verbal repetition of the Name, if it is slow and thoughtful, makes us pass to mental prayer and disposes the soul to contemplation.

II. The Practice of the Invocation of the Name

And I will wait on thy name.

Psalm 52:9.

6. The invocation of the Name may be practised anywhere and at any time. We can pronounce the Name of Jesus in the streets, in the place of our work, in our room, in church, etc. We can repeat the Name while we walk. Besides that "free" use of the Name, not determined or limited by any rule, it is good to set apart certain times and certain places for a "regular" invocation of the Name. One who is advanced in that way of prayer may dispense with such arrangements. But they are an almost necessary condition for beginners.

7. If we daily assign a certain time to the invocation of the Name (besides the "free" invocation which should be as frequent as possible), the invocation ought to be practised — circumstances allowing — in a lonely and quiet place: "Thou, when thou prayest, enter into thine inner chamber, and, when thou hast shut thy door, pray to thy Father which is in secret."[1] The bodily posture does not matter much. One may walk, or sit down, or lie, or kneel. The best posture is the one which affords most physical quiet and inner concentration. One may be helped by a physical attitude expressing humbleness and worship.

8. Before beginning to pronounce the Name of Jesus, establish peace and recollection within yourself and ask for the inspiration and guidance of the Holy Ghost. "No man can say that Jesus is the

Lord, but by the Holy Ghost.''[2] The Name of Jesus cannot really enter a heart that is not being filled by the cleansing breath and the flame of the Spirit. The Spirit himself will breathe and light in us the Name of the Son.

9. Then simply begin. In order to walk one must take a first step; in order to swim one must throw oneself into the water. It is the same with the invocation of the Name. Begin to pronounce it with adoration and love. Cling to it. Repeat it. Do not think that you are invoking the Name; think only of Jesus himself. Say his Name slowly, softly and quietly.

10. A common mistake of beginners is to wish to associate the invocation of the Holy Name with inner intensity or emotion. They try to say it with great force. But the Name of Jesus is not to be shouted, or fashioned with violence, even inwardly. When Elijah was commanded to stand before the Lord, there was a great and strong wind, but the Lord was not in the wind; and after the wind an earthquake, but the Lord was not in the earthquake; and after the earthquake a fire, but the Lord was not in the fire. After the fire came a still small voice, "And it was so, when Elijah heard it, that he wrapped his face in his mantle, and went out, and stood ..."[3] Strenuous exertion and the search for intensity will be of no avail. As you repeat the Holy Name, gather quietly, little by little, your thoughts and feelings and will around it; gather around it your whole being. Let the Name penetrate your soul as a drop of oil spreads out and impregnates a cloth. Let nothing of yourself escape. Surrender your whole self and enclose it within the Name.

11. Even in the act of invocation of the Name, its literal repetition ought not to be continuous. The Name pronounced may be extended and prolonged in seconds or minutes of silent rest and attention. The repetition of the Name may be likened to the beating of wings by which a bird rises into the air. It must never be laboured and forced, or hurried, or in the nature of a flapping. It must be gentle, easy, and — let us give to this word its deepest meaning — graceful. When the bird has reached the desired height it glides in its flight, and only beats its wing from time to time in order to stay in the air. So the soul, having attained to the thought of Jesus and filled herself with the memory of him may discontinue the repetition of the Name and rest in Our Lord. The repetition will only be resumed when other thoughts threaten to crowd out the thought of Jesus. Then the invocation will start again in order to gain fresh impetus.

12. Continue this invocation for as long as you wish or as you can. The prayer is naturally interrupted by tiredness. Then do not

insist. But resume it at any time and wherever you may be, when you feel again so inclined. In time you will find that the Name of Jesus will spontaneously come to your lips and almost continuously be present to your mind, though in a quiescent and latent manner. Even your sleep will be impregnated with the Name and memory of Jesus. "I sleep, but my heart waketh."[4]

13. When we are engaged in the invocation of the Name, it is natural that we should hope and endeavour to reach some "positive" or "tangible" result, *i.e.*, to feel that we have established a real contact with the person of Our Lord: "If I may but touch his garment, I shall be whole."[5] This blissful experience is the desired climax of the invocation of the Name: "I will not let thee go, except thou bless me."[6] But we must avoid an over-eager longing for such experiences; religious emotion may easily become a disguise for some dangerous kind of greed and sensuousness. Let us not think that, if we have spent a certain time in the invocation of the Name without "feeling" anything, our time has been wasted and our effort unfruitful. On the contrary this apparently barren prayer may be more pleasing to God than our moments of rapture, because it is pure from any selfish quest for spiritual delight. It is the prayer of the plain and naked will. We should therefore persevere in assigning every day some regular and fixed time to the invocation of the Name, even if it seems to us that this prayer leaves us cold and dry; and such an earnest exertion of the will, such a sober "waiting" on the Name cannot fail to bring us some blessing and strength.

14. Moreover, the invocation of the Name seldom leaves us in a state of dryness. Those who have some experience of it agree that it is very often accompanied by an inner feeling of joy, warmth and light. One has an impression of moving and walking in the light. There is in this prayer no heaviness, no languishing, no struggling. "Thy name is as ointment poured forth ... Draw me; we will run after thee."[7]

III. The Invocation of the Name as a Spiritual Way

I will strengthen them in the Lord,
and they shall walk up and down in his name.

Zechariah 10:12.

15. The invocation of the Name of Jesus may be simply an episode on our spiritual way (an episode is, etymologically, something that happens "on the way"). Or it may be for us *a* way, one spiritual way

among others. Or it may be *the* way, the spiritual way which we definitely and predominantly (if not exclusively) choose. In other terms the invocation of the Name may be for us either a transitory act, a prayer which we use for a time and leave it for others; or — more than an act — a method which we continuously use, but in addition to other forms and methods of prayer; or the method around which we ultimately build and organize our whole spiritual life. It all depends on our personal call, circumstances and possibilities. Here we are only concerned with "beginners," with those who wish to acquire the first notions about that prayer and a first contact with the Holy Name, and also with those who, having had this first contact, wish to enter "the way of the Name." As to those who are already able to use the invocation of the Name as a method or as the only method, they do not need our advice.

16. We must not come to the invocation of the Name through some whim or arbitrary decision of our own. We must be called to it, led to it by God. If we try to use the invocation of the Name as our main spiritual method, this choice ought to be made out of obedience to a very special vocation. A spiritual practice and much more a spiritual system grounded on a mere caprice will miserably collapse. So we should be moved towards the Name of Jesus under the guidance of the Holy Spirit; then the invocation of the Name will be in us a fruit of the Spirit itself.

17. There is no infallible sign that we are called to the way of the name. There may be, however, some indications of this call, which we ought to consider humbly and carefully. If we feel drawn towards the invocation of the Name, if this practice produces in us an increase of charity, purity, obedience and peace, if the use of other prayers even is becoming somewhat difficult, we may, not unreasonably, assume that the way of the Name is open to us.

18. Anyone who feels the attraction of the way of the Name ought to be careful not to depreciate other forms of prayer. Let us not say: "The invocation of the Name is the best prayer." The best prayer is for everybody the prayer to which he or she is moved by the Holy spirit, whatever prayer it may be. He who practises the invocation of the Name must also curb the temptation of an indiscreet and premature propaganda on behalf of this form of prayer. Let us not hasten to say to God: "I will declare thy name unto thy brethren,"[8] if he is not especially entrusting us with this mission. We should rather humbly keep the secrets of the Lord.

19. What we may say with soberness and truth is this. The invocation of the Name of Jesus simplifies and unifies our spiritual life. No prayer is simpler than this "one-word prayer" in which the

Holy Name becomes the only focus of the whole life. Complicated methods often tire and dissipate thought. But the Name of Jesus easily gathers everything into itself. It has a power of unification and integration. The divided personality which could say: "My name is legion, for we are many"[9] will recover its wholeness in the sacred Name: "*Unite* my heart to fear thy name."[10]

20. The invocation of the Name of Jesus ought not to be understood as a "mystical way" which might spare us the ascetical purifications. There is no short cut in spiritual life. The way of the Name implies a constant watch over our souls. Sin has to be avoided. Only there are two possible attitudes in this respect. Some may guard their mind, memory and will in order to say the Holy Name with greater recollection and love. Others will say the Holy Name in order to be more recollected and whole-hearted in their love. To our mind the latter is the better way. The Name itself is a means of purification and perfection, a touchstone, a filter through which our thoughts, words and deeds have to pass to be freed from their impurities. None of them ought to be admitted by us until we pass them *through* the Name, — and the Name excludes all sinful elements. Only that will be received which is compatible with the Name of Jesus. We shall fill our hearts to the brim with the Name and thought of Jesus, holding it carefully, like a precious vessel, and defending it against all alien tampering and admixture. This is a severe asceticism. It requires a forgetfulness of self, a dying to self, as the Holy Name grows in our souls: "He must increase, but I must decrease."[11]

21. We have to consider the invocation of the Holy Name in relation to other forms of prayer. Of liturgical prayer and of the prayers fixed by some Community rule we shall say nothing, as we are only concerned here with individual and private prayer. We do not disparage or undervalue in the least liturgical prayer and the prayers settled by obedience. Their corporate character and their very fixity render them extremely helpful. But it is for Churchmen and Community members to ascertain whether or how far the invocation of the Name of Jesus is compatible, in their own case, with the official formularies. Questions may be raised about some other forms of individual prayer. What about the "dialogue prayer," in which we listen and speak to God? What about the purely contemplative and wordless prayer, "prayer of quiet" and "prayer of union?" Must we leave these for the invocation of the Holy Name, or inversely? Or should we use both? The answer must be left for God to give in each individual case. In some rare cases the divine call to the invocation of the Name may be exclusive of all other forms of prayer.

But we think that, generally speaking, the way of the Name is broad and free; it is, in most cases, perfectly compatible with moments of listening to the inner Word and answering it and with intervals of complete inner silence. Besides we must never forget that the best form of prayer which we can make at any given moment is that to which we are moved by the Holy Spirit.

22. The advice and discreet guidance of some spiritual "elder" who has a personal experience of the way of the Name may very often be found useful by the beginner. We personally would recommend resort to some such conductor. It is, however, not indispensible. "When the Spirit of truth is come, he will guide you into all truth."[12].

Footnotes:

1. Matthew 6:6.
2. I. Corinthians 12:3.
3. I. Kings 19:13.
4. Song of Songs 5:2.
5. Matthew 9:21.
6. Genesis 32:26.
7. Song of Songs 1:3-4.
8. Psalm 22:22.
9. Mark 5:9.
10. Psalm 86:11.
11. John 3:30.
12. John 16:13.

Prayer

C.S. Lewis

C.S. Lewis, who died in 1963, is probably the best-known modern Christian writer. His professional training was in philosophy, but despite his important work in his own field he was best known as a lay theologian and fantasist. His many books include The Narnia Chronicles, The Great Divorce, Till We Have Faces, Mere Christianity, The Problem of Pain, The Four Loves, *and* Letters to Malcolm: Chiefly on Prayer *from which this excerpt is taken.*

Of the two difficulties you mention I think that only one is often a practical problem for believers. The other is in my experience usually raised by people who are attacking Christianity.

The ideal opening for their attacks — if they know the Bible — is the phrase in Philippians about "making your request known to God." I mean, the words *making known* bring out most clearly the apparent absurdity with which they charge us. We say that we believe God to be omniscient; yet a great deal of prayer seems to consist of giving him information. And indeed we have been reminded by Our Lord too not to pray as if we forgot the omniscience — "for your heavenly Father knows you need all these things."

This is final against one very silly sort of prayer. I have heard a man offer a prayer for a sick person which really amounted to a diagnosis followed by advice as to how God should treat the patient. And I have heard prayers nominally for peace, but really so concerned for various devices which the petitioner believed to be means to peace, that they were open to the same criticism.

But even when that kind of thing is ruled out, the unbeliever's objection remains. To confess our sins before God is certainly to tell Him what He knows much better than we. And also, any petition is a kind of telling. If it does not strictly exclude the belief that God knows our need, it at least seems to solicit His attention. Some traditional formulae make that implication very clear: "Hear us, good Lord" — "O let thine ears consider well the voice of my complaint." As if, though God does not need to be informed, He does need, and even rather frequently, to be reminded. But we cannot really believe that degrees of attention, and therefore of inattention, and therefore of something like forgetfulness, exist in the Absolute Mind. I presume that only God's attention keeps me (or anything else) in existence at all.

What, then, are we really doing? Our whole conception of, so to call it, the prayer-situation depends on the answer.

We are always completely, and therefore equally, known to God. That is our destiny whether we like it or not. But though this knowledge never varies, the quality of our being known can. A school of thought holds that "freedom is willed necessity." Never mind if they are right or not. I want this idea only as an analogy. Ordinarily, to be known by God is to be, for this purpose, in the category of things. We are like earthworms, cabbages, and nebulae, objects of divine knowledge. But when we (a) become aware of the fact — the present fact, not the generalisation — and (b) assent with all our will to be so known, then we treat ourselves, in relation to God, not as things but as persons. We have unveiled. Not that any veil could have baffled this sight. The change is in us. The passive changes to the active. Instead of merely being known, we show, we tell, we offer ourselves to view.

To put ourselves thus on a personal footing with God could, in itself and without warrant, be nothing but presumption and illusion. But we are taught that it is not; that it is God who gives us that footing. For it is by the Holy Spirit that we cry "Father." By unveiling, by confessing our sins and "making known" our requests, we assume the high rank of persons before Him. And He, descending, becomes a Person to us.

But I should not have said "becomes." In Him there is no becoming. He reveals Himself as Person: or reveals that in Him which is Person. For — dare one say it? in a book it would need pages of qualification and insurance — God is in some measure to a man as that man is to God. The door in God that opens is the door he knocks at. (At least, I think so, usually.) The Person in Him — He is more than a person — meets those who can welcome or at least face it. He speaks as "I" when we truly call Him "Thou." (How good Buber is!)

This talk of "meeting" is, no doubt, anthropomorphic; as if God and I could be face to face, like two fellow-creatures, when in reality

He is above me and within me and below me and all about me. That is why it must be balanced by all manner of metaphysical and theological abstractions. But never, here or anywhere else, let us think that while anthropomorphic images are a concession to our weakness, the abstractions are the literal truth. Both are equally concessions; each singly misleading, and the two together mutually corrective. Unless you sit to it very tightly, continually murmuring "Not thus, not thus, neither is this Thou," the abstraction is fatal. It will make the life of lives inanimate and the love of loves impersonal. The *naif* image is mischievous chiefly in so far as it holds unbelievers back from conversion. It does believers, even at its crudest, no harm. What soul ever perished for believing that God the Father really has a beard?

Your question is one which, I think, really gets in pious people's way. It was, you remember, "How important must a need or desire be before we can properly make it the subject of a petition?" *Properly*, I take it, here means either "without irreverence" or "without silliness," or both.

When I'd thought about it for a bit, it seemed to me that there are really two questions involved.

1. How important must an object be before we can, without sin and folly, allow our desire for it to become a matter of serious concern to us? This, you see, is a question about what old writers call our "frame;" that is, our "frame of mind."

2. Granted the existence of such a serious concern in our minds, can it always be properly laid before God in prayer?

We all know the answer to the first of these in theory. We must aim at what St. Augustine (is it?) calls "ordinate loves." Our deepest concern should be for the first things, and our next deepest for second things, and so on down to zero — to total absence of concern for things that are not really good, nor means to good, at all.

Meantime, however, we want to know not how we should pray if we were perfect but how we should pray being as we now are. And if my idea of prayer as "unveiling" is accepted, we have already answered this. It is no use to ask God with factitious earnestness for A when our whole mind is in reality filled with the desire for B. We must lay before Him what is in us, not what ought to be in us.

Even an intimate human friend is ill-used if we talk to him about one thing while our mind is really on another, and even a human friend will soon become aware when we are doing so. You yourself came to see me a few years ago when the great blow had fallen upon me. I tried to talk to you as if nothing were wrong. You saw through it in five minutes. Then I confessed. And you said things which made me ashamed of my attempt at concealment.

It may well be that the desire can be laid before God only as a sin to be repented; but one of the best ways of learning this is to lay it before God. Your problem, however, was not about sinful desires in that sense; rather, about desires, intrinsically innocent and sinning, if at all, only by being stronger than the trivality of their object warrants. I have no doubt at all that if they are the subject of our thoughts they must be the subject of our prayers — whether in penitence or in petition or in a little of both: penitence for the excess, yet petition for the thing we desire.

If one forcibly excludes them, don't they wreck all the rest of our prayers? If we lay all the cards on the table, God will help us to moderate the excesses. But the pressure of things we are trying to keep out of our mind is a hopeless distraction. As someone said, "No noise is so emphatic as one you are trying not to listen to."

The ordinate frame of mind is one of the blessings we must pray for, not a fancy-dress we must put on when we pray.

And perhaps, as those who do not turn to God in petty trials will have no *habit* or such resort to help them when the great trials come, so those who have not learned to ask Him for childish things will have less readiness to ask Him for great ones. We must not be too high-minded. I fancy we may sometimes be deterred from small prayers by a sense of our own dignity rather than of God's.

The Jonas Experience

Noel Dermot O'Donoghue

Noel Dermot O'Donoghue is a member of the Order of Discalced Carmelites. He has lectured throughout the British Isles and in Australia. He is the author of Heaven in Ordinarie, *from which the following essay was taken. Here O'Donoghue looks at an issue which has not been written about frequently enough — the experience of genuine desolation and despair, as a phenomenon encountered in the spiritual life.*

1. The Final Darkness

In what is perhaps the most remarkable passage in her autobiography St. Thérèse of Lisieux speaks of the absolute and unrelenting quality of the darkness which oppressed her spirit during the last eighteen months of her life. She is addressing Mother Gonzague (for whom the later part of her manuscript was written) and she used the idiom by which spiritual experiences were communicated in the milieu of the Lisieux Carmel, an idiom in which all experiences came out as equally deep and equally shallow. But she uses this idiom with a difference.

"I get tired of the darkness all around me, and try to refresh my jaded spirits with the thoughts of that bright country where my hopes lie; and what happens? It is worse torment than ever; the darkness itself seems to borrow, for the sinners who live in it, the gift of speech. I hear its mocking accents; 'It's all a dream, this talk of a heavenly country, bathed in light, scented with delicious perfumes, and of a God who made it all, who is to be your possession in eternity!' You really believe, do you, that the mist which hangs about you will clear away later on? All right, all right, go on longing for death! But death will make nonsense of your hopes; it will only mean a night darker than ever, the night of mere non-existence."[1]

The night of mere non-existence, *la nuit du néant*: this is not a pious cliché, nor was it, when Thérèse penned it, a faded phrase. But to our post existentialist eyes it may *look* faded, as it may sound commonplace to our ears. Let me say then, at once, that it tells of an experience which no man or woman can undergo without the kind of horror and dismay which has strong physical repercussions.

There is nothing easier than to *imagine* this experience without actually undergoing it. It is no less easy to undergo it in such a way that faith and hope take away its cruel and terrible power. But to face it *really*, to enter truly into that darkness in which all light has failed, in which the negation becomes massive and eternal, the negation of all that stands for life and comfort and cheer, in which memory is no more than a further deepening of what is not in the depths of what is no more, nevermore, never more forever ... Oh, yes, all this, too, is marvelous as a game, as the rhetoric of the expert in depth-experience, preaching a retreat for advanced spirits, writing, as I am here, for those looking (very genuinely) for spiritual enlightenment. Even Thérèse writing about it is not *within* it, as she writes, though she is looking down into the abyss and feeling still some of its deathly chill. She conveys something of this chill and something of this uttermost panic in these few words, enough to tell all perhaps to those who have been there or have looked into the depths and fled, like Blake's Thel, "backward into the vale of Har."

Thérèse could have said more, and I think it is clear enough that she wanted to say more to express the truth of the situation, for she loved the truth dearly, even as she looked into the abyss. But she was writing for a woman of limited range (who felt *she* herself had explored all possible spiritual depths) and she did not want to disturb her, or other simple pious souls who might read the manuscript. A recent book, *La Passion de Thérèse de Lisieux* by Guy Gaucher [2] has opened up for us the dimensions of the agony covered by this brief passage in the autobiography and suggests, even imposes, the personal effort of understanding Thérèse more fully at this point. There can be no question of improving on what she has to say, much less question of correcting it in any way. Rather do I wish to attempt a kind of exegesis of this one brief phrase "the night of mere non-existence." I want to invite the reader, if *he will*, to look steadily into that swirling darkness which this phrase discovers or uncovers.

Three aspects of Thérèse's final darkness we must keep in mind if we are to *see* this darkness; her feeling of utter solitude, her fear of going mad, her fancy that she might be buried while still alive. [3]

But, first, let us try to see the light which led Thérèse into this darkness, the light which led her into Carmel and along that very steep and very narrow path which over the last rise, so to speak, plunged downwards into that final terrible darkness, the "cliff of sheer fall, no-man-fathomed" of which Hopkins was to speak.

2. The Little Way

About fifty years ago two Freudian psychiatrists published an analysis of Thérèse's character and projects as revealed by *The Story of a Soul.*[4] They saw her love for her father as central to her existence, and with this an ambivalence towards her mother — we know that as a child she wished her mother dead[5] — which resolved itself in the decision to live within her mother; where she would become fully united with her father.

All this is put forward in a Freudian idiom which has by now lost its freshness, and its power to shock. One can don these Freudian spectacles and look at any story of any life and come up with the same kind of explanation. Yet the Freudian account does place the spotlight on an aspect of Thérèse's home and family that makes many if not most of the readers of her life uneasy if it does not turn them away entirely. There is something strange and oppressive, humanly speaking, about that household of a pious father and five daughters which, apart from the odd visit of the Guerin cousins, is self-sufficient, self-concerned, self-absorbed. Once a young priest visited there and felt his visit was such an intrusion that he never came back. One by one these young women passed out of this strange enclosed atmosphere into the equally strange atmosphere of the Lisieux Carmel which was dominated by a matriarchal woman, Mary Gonzaga. Thérèse made this transition, it must be remembered, at the age of sixteen.

It was within this world, in this psychological atmosphere that the Little Way emerged. It was in this soil that it grew.

All very sweet and comfortable it might seem. But in truth it was bitter, a world of cruel paradoxes. At the end of her life Thérèse pointed to a little bottle of brightly coloured medicine and said "that looks so attractive but it is very bitter — my life has been like that."[6]

In whatever terms we express it — and I think it would be equally unjust to rule out the Freudian statement as to make it central — we can say that Thérèse had to face the problem of coming to terms with an emotional world within herself which was full of pitfalls and destructive possibilities. And she was wise enough to know that she could not traverse this world with the aid of the maps available to her in Carmel. She had to find a way of her own. She found this and she called it "the little way."

She found "the little way" in the Scriptures, mainly in the New Testaments though some texts from the Old Testaments were also important. She saw that the figure of the child was central to the message of Jesus (how consistently dogmatic theologies overlook this!). This she saw clearly and as it were exclusively through her deep relationship with her father, the central human relationship that, so to speak, shaped her heart and defined her being. She saw that the father-child relationship is the very basis of the New Testament, being at once the central dynamism of the life of Jesus and the pivot of his ethical teaching. In this relationship the father is entirely loving and full of delicate understanding. Against all other notions of the deity Thérèse clung to this with unbreakable stubbornness. The only way that it might be put in question was through the very existence of God being put in question, and that is what happened at the end.

The little way was for Thérèse the way of the child who runs to its father's arms with complete trust. It might seem easy to imitate, and in fact Thérèse saw it as a way for "little souls," but it is only easy *as long as the father counts for everything,* as long as one's treasure is fully and exclusively in the father's keeping. This involves total detachment, and total detachment is not possible to "little souls" as long as the word "little" is taken as involving deficiency in detachment. The detached spirit deserves most of all the title of greatness, and so Thérèse's little way is an invitation addressed only to those who seek true greatness. It is a way for the truly heroic, a way that puts all pseudo-heroisms in question. Yet it does, and this must be said, run in the same direction as all other true ways and does *not* put a question after any way of true heroism no matter how different. For its rightness arises from the fact that it is a truly heroic way, involving full attachment to the *all*, and full detachment from all else.

But Thérèse knew that, even though the Father is kind and loving, yet He makes absolute demands. Indeed she understood intuitively from the beginning, and this intuition never left her, that it was precisely this fathering love that generated these absolute demands. She understood that she could not be taken up to where the Father is, that she could not enter into that union with the Father for which her whole being yearned unless she were ready to be taken beyond all finite limits and all the security and comfort of the human. She knew that she had to go by way of Gethsemane and Calvary, that the image of Jesus crucified, the visage of Christ in agony which the piety of her time spoke of as the Holy Face.[7]

So she chose to be known as *Thérèse of the Child Jesus and of the Holy Face*, and at the end it was the image and likeness of the Face of the Suffering Christ that came to be imprinted on the very substance of her being.

3. The Jonas Experience

Some years ago an Irishman gained some fame by staying in an underground box or coffin for several days. He had friends above ground with whom he was in contact, and he had but to speak into a tube to put an end to the ordeal. He must have had his moments of panic, but he did not really have to enter the deeper panic of the man who is trapped in the depths and has to wait for death. It is said that if death delays he will first go mad. It is not easy to say what "going mad" might mean in such circumstances. Perhaps it means that he will try to hasten death — if he can. He will perhaps cry out in despair.

But if he is a man of strong faith he will await death calmly, death or release. He will pray with some knowledge that God knows his plight and loves him and will surely bring about what is best. After panic and near-despair there will, perhaps, come a great peace and even a great joy in the immensity of the divine purposes.

Yes, but where is God in the silence and darkness, in the laboured beatings of the heart? Where is the *idea* of God in this uttermost emptiness? Perhaps after all the ultimate truth is not light and goodness but darkness and horror? Surely this terrible happening, this extreme anguish of the poor naked human spirit is proof that there is no God at all or that if there is he is without care of me? "All thy billows and thy waves have passed over me ... The water compassed me about even to the soul ... the bars of the earth have shut me up for ever."[8] So spoke Jonas, and Job too under the silent heavens. It is indeed a note that is struck again and again in the Old Testament. But always the Lord comes to save, and is as it were thus, by this extremity, defined in the fulness of his saviourhood. Jesus comes as the one who saves, the God who saves. Yet he is also Jonas and he enters into the darkness of Gethsemane and the darkness of the tomb.

But we miss the whole point if we think that the release, the happy outcome, is somehow present to the man who enters into these depths. That would be to destroy both the experience and the release from it. It is true that the author of Jonas attaches a note of firm confidence to the prayer from the depths and shows us Jonas as speedily released; so too Job holds on stubbornly to his belief in an ultimate goodness. And it is true that the man who is thus utterly alone and utterly forsaken may have the inner light and strength of faith and hope.

But this, too, may fail, or, if you like, be taken away, as the final test. And this test is almost too awful to think of. Few have described it. Perhaps few have experienced it.

The most complete and penetrating description of this state is that to be found in the second book of *The Dark Night of the Soul* of St. John of the Cross. He takes up the imagery of the book of Jonas — indeed, here as elsewhere, his claim is that he is doing no more than interpreting the mystical undercurrent of Scripture — combining it with passages from Job, Jeremiah and the Psalms. But the voice is entirely his own, and it is clear that he speaks out of abundant personal experience. In this state, he tells us "a man feels very vividly indeed the shadow of death, the sighs of death and the sorrows of hell ... Sometimes this experience is so vivid that it seems to the soul that it sees hell and perdition open before it ... He resembles one who is imprisoned in a dark dungeon, bound hands and feet, and able neither to move, nor see, nor feel any favour from heaven or earth."[9]

Those who know the poetry of Gerard Manley Hopkins can scarcely read this without thinking of "the terrible sonnets;" there is the same sense of ultimate, massive dereliction, of closed space, of frightening featureless depths, of the vanishing of all that might give support or comfort.[10] It must be said also that Hopkins writes from within the experience itself, while in the case of St. John we feel that the experience has been lived through, has been in a sense transcended.

There is an immense gulf between the two states, that of being within the experience and that of being outside it having been in it. What has to be understood is that while the experience lasts the sufferer is indeed in a kind of hell, eternally lost, facing total nothingness, the utter and final annihilation of what Heidegger calls the "ownmost self." Not one ray of hope, not one chink of light.

Above all, the utter loneliness. There is nobody there, nor was there ever, nor will there ever be. Or if there is, far off, Somebody, he is not concerned, or else is positively hostile.

Again it is easy as a game, as something to pretend, a kind of hide and seek. And, of course, mystics, like other lovers, do play such games with the Beloved. But this is something else entirely. Here is sheer, utter panic. Here is horror and dismay, sheer horror, utter dismay. The body shares the spirit's agony. "Horror and dismay overcame him ... and his sweat became as drops of blood falling down upon the ground."[11]

All that is left is prayer. But prayer in a special sense. The prayer of "not my will but thine be done," the prayer of "why hast thou forsaken me." That on the one hand. And on the other the prayer Jesus told his disciples to pray as they waited outside Gethsemane. "Why are you asleep?" he said, "wake up and pray that you be not put to the test."[12]

These two prayers are as it were the intensely painful inhalation and exhalation of a dying man, of the ownmost self in its last agony.

4. Cliffs of Fall Frightful

This is the death of the spirit, and it is this that Thérèse had to undergo as her body died its physical death.

The physical process was itself very painful, *un vrai martyre*, her doctor said. The remedies applied to her tubercular condition were at once extremely painful, utterly humiliating and, as she herself knew, entirely ineffective. She became hyper-sensitive, irritable, plagued by irrational desires and fancies. She had not the consolation of bearing it all patiently, for, to her great chagrin, she would lose patience with people and with their pointless remedies and questionings.[13]

In all this there was spiritual gain, which she was wise enough to appreciate. Why should not the traveller along the "little way" show her poverty in such matters as patience? And in the physical suffering, though she cried out for release, there was the deep sense of the rightness of being fastened with Jesus to the Cross.

But the inner darkness, the agony of the spirit's death was of quite another order. Here "the little way" of trust and self-surrender, of childlike and simple love fails completely, for its object, its centre of reference has disappeared. There is no God; there never was a God, nor will there ever be. It is all illusion, all part of the great foolishness of life. One can indeed continue to make acts of faith and hope but these acts are simply part of the great illusion. All that comes back from the silent heavens is the echo of one's own voice.

If we really want to enter into the world of Thérèse's final darkness we must see and say that here at last is the truth. We can, in total despair, let old Horace speak for us: *maret una nox omnibus*, the one night awaits us all. This dearly-beloved, this poor trembling ownmost self vanishes for ever under the cold stars. Not as a game, not as a fling of rhetoric, not as a preacher's gambit to announce some kind of resurrection, but in cold truth.

O the mind, mind has mountains; cliffs of fall
Frightful, sheer, no-man-fathomed. Hold them cheap
May who ne'er living there.

So Hopkins, as his poetry goes beyond its own creative delight to speak final truth.

As the immortal spirit thus looks its own death in the face the body trembles and shudders, and the cry of final dereliction rises up. *Sine decore*: not so much a cry as a scream, where, as in Edvard Munch's picture, the person dies off into the scream. Nought is left but the scream. This is the ultimate truth.

Munch's picture might well stand as a representation of the last act of the "passion" of Thérèse: alone, in the dark, in a choking panic, facing final despair. The experience itself cut her off from those around her: her sisters could not bear it, and fled to seek release in anguished prayer. They prayed that she might not die in despair.[14] "Ah my *good* God," Thérèse cried again and again, as she looked at the face of uncaring power, as she, in her way, encountered the silent skies of Auschwitz and Hiroshima. "Ah my *good* God," the God of her sheltered youth, of all the facile pieties, the God who was in Jesus, the suffering saviour; — he was no longer there. All that was there was the sheer descent from panic into despair. No wonder that she came to think of suicide, for the test was beyond bearing.[15]

"Put me not to the test;" she must have prayed this prayer, the prayer of the disciples outside the garden. "Father if it be possible let this chalice pass from me, but nevertheless not my will but thine be done." Thérèse would not remain outside the place of agony, with the disciples, asleep or awake. Love, as she knew it, knows no limits of prudence or possiblity, and so she had to enter into the full "horror and dismay" of the test.

From the outside she saw this; she willed this; she felt secure in willing this, for she was dealing with supreme love, supreme goodness. *Within* all was different: there not only was all comfort lacking, but the powers that ruled, not just this world of darkness, but *the* world, were utterly pitiless and remote. This was not just a world ruled by uncaring and relentless power — power that was even farther off than hatred or hostility — a power antagonistic to an all-good Creator. No, what Thérèse (with all true explorers of this spiritual realm) had to face was the disappearance of all good godhead into this uncaring godhead. It is the encounter with final despair. It is the dying of the spirit. And to meet this *really* and with no ray of light from a better world, to know *for certain* that thus it is: this is indeed the final test. Those who most loved Thérèse could not bear to live near this agony: they had to leave the place of agony and pray. This flight too was real. They could not bear the atmosphere of the place of agony where Thérèse desired to be with her Suffering Consort at the end. They had to return to where the disciples waited and prayed, or slept.

That, too, was and is a holy place, perhaps for most of us the limit beyond which we cannot go in our discipleship. We can but watch and pray, that we be not put to that final test, yet withal resting in the Divine will. Perhaps slowly we may learn to breathe that other air and go a little nearer to that inner sanctuary.

5. The Crucible

In their happy times together, in the bright days of her girlhood, Thérèse would call her father "King of France and Navarre." He was her "beloved king," she his "princess." These playful titles come up again and again, and they help us to measure the depth and direction of the affectivity from which the "little way" issued. The Divine Fatherhood was the extension and, as it were, final ground, of this all-absorbing human relationship. This was not just the kind of projection natural to a pious girl; from the beginning Thérèse was a Platonist in the sense that only the eternal and completely grounded had reality for her. She could only give herself fully to an eternal lover, a "heavenly" father.

This elan was deep and narrow and it might easily have sought security in a narrow unreflective Catholicism. It might have produced an efficient Mistress of Novices but no more than that. The great breakthrough came with the mental breakdown of the "beloved king," a breakdown that was final and lasted till his death. From the breaking of the human image the Divine reality painfully emerged, the father not just of Thérèse and her family but equally of all the sisters in the convent, so that to love him was to love them, even, or especially, the tiresome and neurotic ones. This was the challenge Thérèse had to face in the convent, the war she had to win and she faced it soldier-wise (the military image was dear to her; St. Joan was never far from her mind), rejoicing in her victories, learning the lessons of her defeats, so as to turn them into victories. The wounds and travail of this contest became sacrificial gifts to offer the beloved, the Father present in his Son Jesus, the "Spouse" to whom Thérèse was indissolubly wed through her Carmelite profession of vows.

After six years in Carmel she could say that she had triumphed. That ardent affectivity had broken through the constricting limits of her family, and now radiated to the whole world, for her immediate Carmelite environment was the concentration of all possible challenges, a refining crucible wherein that primary elan could only be diminished and quenched or immeasurably strengthened. Only those who have experience of a small closed community can realize fully the greatness of this achievement and what kind of radiance the famous "smile" of Thérèse really sent forth to those who lived with her or met her.

She had won the victory and when she knew that she was to die she was filled with joy. Death would simply be a release into the fulness of that love that was already consuming her. She would have to face physical suffering, but that itself was but the presence of the transforming fire of love.

Then the real darkness came down and she had to go the way of Job and Jonas, of Jesus in Gethsemane. Panic, loneliness, despair: the uttermost reality of the undoing of the ownmost self. Up to the point where even her valiant sister, Pauline, fled in dismay and terror.

This was the final test of love, where only love remained and love had no other foundations but itself, itself as evanescent, as dying in the death of all else, love in its final nakedness and purity. The "little way" vanished into its own littleness, being no more than a whispered word that died away into the eternal silence.

6. Victory

Then, at the end, at the very end, peace, joy, fulfilment. It was as if that final assault of darkness and all the terror of non-existence had opened up a great new world that awaited the dawn of God's love, a world somehow large enough to hold it all. It was about five o'clock of the evening of 30 September 1897, a day of heavy rain, the day in which the agony of Thérèse had entered its final, most terrifying phase. A certain peace heralded the end and the community gathered around her bed. Her face changed, regaining its former glowing colour and she fixed her eyes on a point above the statute of of the Virgin Mary, that had been placed in her little room, in a kind of ecstasy that lasted "the space of a *Credo*," a look of great joy and a strange majesty and dignity.[16] She was being born into the infinite, into the life of the world, into the lives of all of us.

7. The Birth of Love

It is sometimes said that at the end of her life Thérèse entered into the experience of the atheist. Indeed she herself said that she had come to eat at the table of unbelievers. But we must be careful not to confuse this with the Jonas experience or, better, the Gethsemane experience which has been in question here. Central to this latter experience is a sense of loss and forsakenness. It is only because one has, somehow, opened out to the (positive) Infinite that one discovers within that space whereby the awful chasm of the negative infinite opens up. There can, of course, be professed atheists or unbelievers who have nevertheless opened up to the greatness of reality, feeling with Karl Jaspes, the call of the "encompassing," and for such people this kind of experience is, so to speak, available. Certainly one can think of a Sartre or a Heidegger as undergoing it — indeed I have been forced to use Heidegger's phrase "ownmost self" to describe the kind of inner destruction the experience brings. The "bread of unbelievers" (or at least *a certain kind* of it) may perhaps be sustaining when all is said, at least, to continue the metaphor, for those of specially sturdy spiritual constitution.

But that emergence at the end from the dark waters? Is that also available to the unbeliever? Is it here perhaps that the underground stream of faith surfaces again? Perhaps. But I prefer to recall that for Thérèse one thing alone remained when all was gone: love. Love, naked, poor, unsupported by the promise of future joy and glory. It was, I think, this that issued forth in power at the end, finding its complete support, its indestructible eternity within itself, where all the time, mysteriously, God was being born again.

Footnotes:

1. Ms. C6v. *Autobiography of a Saint*, tr. by R. Knox, ch. 32.
2. Paris: Desclee, 1973.
3. Gaugher, p. 100 and passim.
4. I. F. Grant Duff, *A Psychoanalytical Study of a Fantasy of St. Thérèse* in *British Journal of Medical Psychology*, 1925. The other psychiatrist is Ernest Jones, to whom Miss Grant Duff acknowledges her debt in a fuller exposition of her thesis in *Imago*, 1934. These articles have recently appeared in a French translation with commentary by Jacques Maitre in *Archives de Sciences Sociales des Religions*, 1976, pp. 109-136.

Footnotes: cont.

5. Knox, ch. 2.
6. Novissima Verba, 30 July.
7. It has in fact a solid Scriptural foundation in Isaias, 53:2 and 3, as well as in the Passion narratives.
8. Jonas 2: 3.
9. Bk. 2, ch. 6 and ch. 7.
10. See especially *No worst, there is none.*
11. Mark 14: 33; Luke 22: 44.
12. Luke 22: 46.
13. Gaucher, *passim.*
14. Gaucher, p. 113. To them this would seem to die in sin, like Judas.
15. Gaucher, p. 114.
16. See Gaucher, p. 228 for a careful analysis of the statements concerning this "ecstasy" of Thérèse at death.

Mysticism in Action

William Johnston

*William Johnston, former director of the In-
stitute of Oriental Religions and Professor of
Religious Studies at Sophia University in Tokyo,
is a member of the Jesuit order. Johnston's work
draws on both Eastern and Western mystical
traditions, and his books include* Silent Music,
Christian Zen, The Mirror Mind, *and* The Inner
Eye of Love. *Here Johnston deals with the common accusation that mysticism and social action are mutually exclusive.*

I.

Critics of mysticism frequently point to the immense social problems of our day — the hunger, the air pollution, the social injustice,
the racial discrimination, the political corruption, the danger of
nuclear war, the exploitation of the rich by the poor, the torture of
political prisoners. And then they ask about mysticism. How will
this help solve contempory problems? Is it not a luxury to retire to
the desert while large sections of humanity face utter destruction?
Surely the first duty of modern man is to stretch out a helping hand
to his fellow-men and women, to alleviate their suffering, to bring
peace and happiness to the world.

These statements and these questions are all very reasonable. Of
course we must marshal our forces to help suffering humanity and
to build a better world. The only problem is: how? Activists
sometimes overlook the undeniable fact that unenlightened, unre-
generate, unconverted men and women can do nothing to solve the
vast problems with which we are confronted. Not only will they do
nothing but they may do immense damage. They may line their
own pockets with the money which should go to the poor (and, alas,
we have seen this happen very often); or they may be carried away
by passionate anger and violently create more problems than they

solve; or they may simply lack the depth and vision to see the roots of the problems. The weakness of human nature is something we cannot with impunity overlook. Buddhism teaches that prior to enlightenment we are in illusion — we are lost in the woods and don't even see the footprints of the ox. And then Christianity teaches about original sin. In either case, to work for humanity one must be enlightened. What the modern world needs is enlightened men and women.

Once enlightened we no longer rely on our little ego but on a power which is greater than ourselves. "Apart from me," says Jesus, "you can do nothing" (John 15:5). And Paul, carried away to boast that he has laboured more than all the others, is forced to correct himself: "it was not I, but the grace of God which is with me" I Corinthians 15:10). Yes, Paul. You never said a truer word. It was not your strength; it was a greater power within you to which you surrendered. Your strength was in weakness. Your action was rooted in non-action.

And so if we are in any way to solve the problems of our day we must rely on the power of another, not on our own power. And this is non-action which, I have tried to say, is the most powerful action of all. It manifests itself in the human heart as a blind stirring of love, as a living flame of love. Sometimes, it is true, this inner fire drives people into solitude where they intercede for mankind and unleash a power which shakes the universe. But the same inner fire drives others into the midst of action with a passionate love for justice and a willingness to die for their convictions. Indeed, this flame of love may suddenly become dynamic in the heart of a solitary — who suddenly discovers that he is called to action and that he cannot refuse the invitation. Such was the shepherd-prophet Amos who protests: "I am no prophet, nor a prophet's son; but I am a herdsman, and a dresser of sycamore trees, and the Lord took me from following the flock, and the Lord said to me, 'Go, prophesy to my people Israel' " (Amos 7:14,15). Poor Amos! Like Jeremiah and Jonah he did not want to be involved in tumultuous action; but the inner flame, the inner voice, drove him on and, under its influence, he thundered against the rich:

Hear this, you who trample upon the needy
and bring the poor of the land to an end

(Amos 8:4)

Here is the action which is the overflow of mysticism. It is filled with compassion for the poor and needy and underprivileged.

II.

I have said that the mystical flame sometimes drives hermits or solitaries into action. But I can immediately hear the objection: "But the mystic who has spent long periods in solitude knows nothing about the world. How, then, can he solve its problems? Let him subscribe to *Time* and *Newsweek*. Let him read the *New York Times*. Or, better still, let him take a guided tour around Calcutta and be 'exposed to the poor.' Then we'll listen to him."

Well, well. I wonder. Let us never underestimate the wisdom of the desert. For the fact is that the person who has spent long periods in authenic prayer and meditation knows about the suffering of the world because he has experienced it all within himself. How often has a repentant sinner, filled with remorse for his iniquities and failures, gone to the solitary monk to confess his crimes — and, lo and behold, he has found someone who understands the whole story. For the monk has experienced it all within himself — in another way. He has met the devil and seen his own awful weakness and potentiality for evil. It does not shock him to hear about murder and rape and violence — and he is filled with compassion for the weakness of a human race to which he himself belongs. Moreover, like Kannon who with that exquisite smile of compassion hears the cries of the poor, the mystic also has in his own way heard the cries of the underprivileged, the downtrodden, the victims of violence and deceit and exploitation — just as Jesus knew it all in Gethsemane. Of course it will do him no harm to read *Time* and *Newsweek* also. And if he does, he will find there things which the authors of the articles did not realize.

In the midst of solitude, then, a person may receive a prophetic vocation like that of Amos. And he may struggle against it. But his struggle will be in vain; and he will be pursued by the inexorable words: "To all to whom I send you you shall go, and whatever I command you you shall speak. Be not afraid of them, for I am with you to deliver you, says the Lord" (Jeremiah 1:7). And so he goes into action and his action is fruitful because the Lord is with him and because he sees problems at their root and in their totality. His enlightened eye penetrates through the lines of *Time* and *Newsweek* to the basic cause of all our problems which is that mysterious reality which Christians call sin and Buddhists call blindness and ignorance.

I have spoken of the solitary who is called to action. But the mystic in action need not have been solitary. He may (and this is the Ignatian ideal) be a person who has spent his years in a cycle of contemplation-action-contemplation-action; and in this way he has attained to enlightenment. The important thing is not whether or not he has spent years in solitude. What matters is that he should be enlightened — that his eye of love penetrate beyond the superficial appearances to the root cause of our problems and to the ultimate solution which lies beyond the cloud of unknowing.

But what, you may ask, will he do? And to this I can only answer, as I have previously said, that he will follow the guidance of the inner light. Nor is this an easy task. Because following the light is different from following an idea or an ideology. It demands liberation from ideology so that one can listen to the voice of the beloved which will, at times, run counter to all ideologies. But one must discern that voice; and we find that the true mystic in action is always praying for light, always searching for the way. His initial call points out the general direction, but it does not enlighten every step of the path. Quite often there will be anguish and fear and uncertainty and conflict like that of Jeremiah: "Woe is me, my mother, that you bore me, a man of strife and contention to the whole land!" (Jeremiah 15:10).

This inner light leads in the most surprising ways. Prophetical people are quite unpredictable. Often they are socially unacceptable, strident, exaggerated, apparently unorthodox. Like Jeremiah they are often ridiculed and put in the stocks. Usually they are put to death, either literally or metaphorically. But the distinctive thing is the quality of their love which "bears all things, believes all things, hopes all things, endures all things" (I Corinthians 13:7).

Consequently there is no blueprint to tell us what the mystic in action will do. He might do anything. But, on the other hand, he will have his charisma which he must faithfully follow. And this is true of all of us. We are not called to serve in the same way. "Are all apostles? Are all prophets? Are all teachers? Do all work miracles? Do all possess gifts of healing? Do all speak with tongues? Do all interpret?" (I Corinthians 12:29). We cannot ask that every prophet walk in peace marches or teach the blind or visit the sick or denounce the politically corrupt. Each must follow his own distinctive charisma.

And we must have our ears to the ground to listen for the true prophets, to recognize them, to follow their guidance and not to kill them. This is the great challenge of our day. Around us are prophets and false prophets. By their fruits we shall know them; by their fruits only can we distinguish the authentic from the pretenders. And Paul has spoken of those fruits of the Spirit which are "love, joy, peace, patience, kindness, goodness, faithfulness, gentleness, self-control" (Galatians 5:22). If these are present we should listen to the prophet, even when his words run counter to what we hold sacred and believe.

III.

St. Paul says that the important thing is love. After extolling the various charismatic gifts he goes on to say that what is, or should be, common to them all is love. Without love the gifts are useless. And so he begins his canticle: "If I speak in the tongues of men and of angels, but not have love, I am a noisy gong or a clanging cymbal" (I Corinthians 13:1).

Gandhi recognized this; but in his peculiar circumstances he preferred to speak of non-violence or *ahimsa*. This included compassion for the poor, love of the aggressor, love of justice. It renounced all hatred and use of force; but believed in force of another kind: *satyagraha* means the force of truth.

To build one's activity on love and non-violence demands the greatest inner purification. One must constantly rid one's heart of inordinate desires and fears and anxieties; but above all one must cleanse oneself from anger.

In our day anger seems to be the chief enemy of love and non-violence. By anger I mean the inner violence which lies not only in the conscious but also in the unconscious mind of individuals and of whole nations. This is an inner violence which has sometimes been nurtured by domestic strife in the home; always it is the source of great insecurity, inner fear and awful weakness. This is the anger which may erupt into sexual crimes or irrational murder and terrorism.

Now if I come to recognize the anger which is in me (and this is already great progress in the journey towards human maturity) and if I ask a psychologist what I am to do with my anger, the odds are that he will tell me, among other things, to get it out of my system. "Get it out somehow! Imagine that your enemy is seated beside you and just roar at him — tell him what you feel! Or thump a pillow or a punch-ball or a sack of hay! But get it out!"

Now this may sound a thousand miles away from mystical experience. But in fact it is not. Because in the mystical path anger comes out — it rises to the surface of consciousness. Remember that I spoke of the Buddha sitting serenely in meditation while the beasts roar and the dogs bark. These are manifestations of my hidden anger. As I have already said, I must not make violent efforts to chase them away, neither must I enter into dialogue with them. I simply pay no attention to them — and in doing this I accept them. And then they vanish. In some cases, of course, it may also be necessary to speak about them to a friend or counsellor. But in any case I get them out of my system.

But when this is done, something still remains. And this is *just anger*. In other words, my anger has not been annihilated but has been purified. Now it is the anger of one who has seen, and still sees, real injustice in his own life and in that of others and refuses to countenance such evil. It is an anger which could be more properly called *love of justice* and is accompanied by a willingness to die in the cause of justice. In itself this is nothing other than a mystical experience. It is the living flame of love orientated towards action.

Such was the righteous indignation of the prophets. Such was the anger of one who made a whip and drove the money-changers out of the temple: "Take these things away; you shall not make my Father's house a house of trade" (John 2:16). Gandhi, too, was moved by this just anger: he spoke frequently of marshalling all one's spiritual forces against the oppressor and he fought injustice by fasting, by suffering, by accepting imprisonment and by non-violence.

IV.

From all that has been said and from a perusal of the Fourth Gospel it will be clear that mystical action is chiefly a matter of bearing fruit. It is not a question of frenetic activity, of getting a lot done, of achieving immediate results. Rather is it a question of unrestricted love which goes on and on and on.

Such love always bears fruit. Such love always leads to a union which creates something new. But the new creation may be quite different from what the mystic and his followers expected. His life, like that of Jesus, may end in apparent failure. But when it does, people in another part of the world and perhaps in another era will reap the fruit. For "here the saying holds true, 'One sows and another reaps,' I sent you to reap that for which you did not labour; others have laboured and you have entered into their labour" (John 4:37,38).

Action

Donald P. McNeill, Douglas A. Morrison and Henri J.M. Nouwen

Donald P. McNeill directs the Center for Experimental Learning at the University of Notre Dame. Douglas A. Morrison is director of the Pastoral Center at Catholic University in Washington. Henri J.M. Nouwen, a popular author of many books on the spiritual life, is currently on the faculty of the Harvard Divinity School. In their book Compassion, *from which this selection is drawn, they show the connections between the life of the spirit and the suffering world in which so much needs to be done.*

Here and Now

If the emphasis on prayer were an escape from direct engagement with the many needs and pains of our world, then it would not be a real discipline of the compassionate life. Prayer challenges us to be fully aware of the world in which we live and to present it with all its needs and pains to God. It is this compassionate prayer that calls for compassionate action. The disciple is called to follow the Lord not only into the desert and onto the mountain to pray but also into the valley of tears, where help is needed, and onto the cross, where humanity is in agony. Prayer and action, therefore, can never be seen as contradictory or mutually exclusive. Prayer without action grows into powerless pietism, and action without prayer degegenerates into questionable manipulation. If prayer leads us into a deeper unity with the compassionate Christ, it will always give rise to concrete acts of service. And if concrete acts of service do indeed lead us to a deeper solidarity with the poor, the hungry, the sick, the dying, and the oppressed, they will always give rise to prayer. In prayer we meet Christ, and in him all human suffering. In service we meet people, and in them the suffering Christ.

The discipline of patience reveals itself not only in the way we pray but also on the way we act. Our actions, like our prayers, must be a manifestation of God's compassionate presence in the midst of our world. Patient actions are actions through which the healing, consoling, comforting, reconciling, and unifying love of God can touch the heart of humanity. They are actions through which the fullness of time can show itself and God's justice and peace can guide our world. They are actions by which good news is brought to the poor, liberty to the prisoners, new sight to the blind, freedom to the oppressed, and God's year of favor is proclaimed (Lk 4:18-19). They are actions that remove the fear, suspicion, and power-hungry competition that cause an escalating arms race, an increasing separation between the wealthy and the poor, and an intensifying cruelty between the powerful and the powerless. They are actions that lead people to listen to each other, speak with each other, and heal each other's wounds. In short, they are actions based on a faith that knows God's presence on our lives and wants this presence to be felt by individuals, communities, societies and nations.

Patient action is a hard discipline. Often, our lives get so over-burdened that it takes every bit of energy to survive the day. Then it becomes hard to value the present moment, and we can only dream about a future time and place where everything will be different. We want to move away from the present moment as quickly as possible and create a new situation in which present pains are absent. But such impatient action prevents us from recognizing the possibilities of the moment and thus easily leads us to an intolerant fanaticism. Action as a discipline of compassion requires the willingness to respond to the very concrete needs of the moment.

The Test of Credibility

Probably no New Testament writer is as explicit about the importance of concrete acts of service as James. He writes, "Pure, unspoilt religion, in the eyes of God our Father is this: coming to the help of orphans and widows when they need it, and keeping oneself uncontaminated by the world." (Jm 1:27). With considerable irony, James shows to the "twelve tribes of the Dispersion" — i.e., the Jewish Christians scattered all over the Graeco-Roman world — the importance of concrete acts of service.

Take the case, my brothers, of someone who has never done a single good act but claims that he has faith. Will that faith save him? If one of the brothers or one of the sisters is in need of clothes and has not enough food to live on, and one of you says to them, "I wish you well; keep yourself warm and eat plenty," without giving them these bare necessities of life, then what good is that? Faith is like that: if good works do not go with it, it is quite dead.

(Jm 2:14-17)

James even goes so far as to instruct his readers about how to speak to those who think that merely having faith in God is sufficient.

This is the way you talk to people of that kind: "You say you have faith and I have good deeds; I will prove to you that I have faith by showing you my good deeds — now you prove to me that you have faith without any good deeds to show. You believe in the one God — that is creditable enough, but the demons have the same belief, and they tremble with fear. Do realise, you senseless man, that faith without good deeds is useless."

(Jm 2:18-20)

After showing how in the lives of Abraham and Rahab faith and deeds work together, James concludes, "A body dies when it is separated from the spirit, and in the same way faith is dead if it is separated from good deeds" (Jm 2:26).

It is obvious that James does little more than restate in a new context Jesus' emphasis on concrete acts of service. When the disciples of John the Baptist ask Jesus if he is "the one who is to come," Jesus points to his actions, "the blind see again, the lame walk, lepers are cleansed, and the deaf hear, the dead are raised to life, the Good News is proclaimed to the poor" (Lk 7:22-23). His actions are the source of his credibility. The same is true of his disciples. Jesus wants them to be people of action. He leaves little doubt about his opinion, " ... the one who listens and does nothing is like the man who built his house on soil, with no foundation: as soon as the river bore down on it, it collapsed; and what a ruin that house became!" (Lk 6:49). With great persistence, Jesus stresses that the test of true discipleship lies not in words but in actions: "It is not those who say to me, 'Lord, Lord,' who will enter the kingdom of heaven, but the person who does the will of my Father

in heaven" (Mt 7:21-22). Indeed, prayer must yield specific fruits.
The final criterion of the value of the Christian life is therefore not
prayer but action. In the "wordy" environment of teachers,
masters, scribes and Pharisees, Jesus wants his followers to
discover for themselves that mere words will not bring them into
the kingdom.

> What is your opinion? A man had two sons. He went and said
> to the first, "My boy, you go and work in the vineyard today."
> He answered, "I will not go," but afterwards thought better of
> it and went. The man then went and said the same thing to
> the second who answered, "Certainly, sir," but did not go.
> Which of the two did the father's will? "The first," they said.
>
> (Mt 21:28-31)

Should there still exist any question in his hearers' minds, Jesus
erases the vestiges of doubt when he describes the last judgment, in
which concrete acts of compassion are the undeniable signs of
"unspoilt religion" (James). Perhaps nowhere else in the New
Testament do we find the importance of the discipline of action so
clearly presented:

> When the Son of Man comes in his glory, escorted by all the
> angels, then he will take his seat on his throne of glory. All the
> nations will be assembled before him and he will separate
> men from one another as the shepherd separates sheep from
> goats. He will place the sheep on his right hand and the goats
> on his left. Then the King will say to those on his right hand,
> "Come, you whom the Father has blessed, take for your
> heritage the kingdom prepared for you since the foundation of
> the world. For I was hungry and you gave me food; I was
> thirsty and you gave me drink; I was a stranger and you made
> me welcome; naked and you clothed me, sick and visited me,
> in prison and you came to see me." Then the virtuous will say
> to him in reply, "Lord, when did we see you hungry and feed
> you; or thirsty and give you drink? When did we see you a
> stranger and make you welcome; naked and clothe you; sick
> or in prison and go to see you?" The King will answer, "I tell
> you solemnly, in so far as you did this to one of the least of
> these brothers of mine, you did it to me." Next he will say to
> those on his left hand, "Go away from me, with your curse
> upon you, to the eternal fire prepared for the devil and his
> angels. For I was hungry and you never gave me food; I was

thirsty and you never gave me anything to drink; I was a stranger and you never made me welcome, naked and you never clothed me, sick and in prison and you never visited me." Then it will be their turn to ask, "Lord, when did we see you hungry and thirsty, a stranger or naked, sick or in prison, and did not come to your help?" Then he will answer, "I tell you solemnly, in so far as you neglected to do this to one of the least of these, you neglected to do it to me." And they will go away to eternal punishment, and the virtuous to eternal life.

(Mt 25:31-46)

This dramatic scene vividly portrays the meaning of the discipline of action. Action with and for those who suffer is the concrete expression of the compassionate life and the final criterion of being a Christian. Such acts do not stand beside the moments of prayer and worship but are themselves such moments. Why? Because Jesus Christ, who did not cling to his divinity, but became as we are, can be found where there are hungry, thirsty, alienated, naked, sick and imprisoned people. Precisely when we live in an ongoing conversation with Christ and allow his Spirit to guide our lives, we will recognize him in the poor, the oppressed and the down-trodden, and will hear his cry and respond to it wherever he reveals himself. Thus, action and prayer are two aspects of the same discipline of patience. Both require that we be present to the suffering world here and now and that we respond to the specific needs of those who make up our world, a world claimed by Jesus Christ as his own. So worship becomes ministry and ministry becomes worship, and all we say and do, ask for or give, becomes a way to the life in which God's compassion can manifest itself.

The Temptation of Activism

The disciples speak of their actions as manifestations of God's active presence. They act not to prove their own power, but to show God's power; they act not to redeem people but to reveal God's redemptive grace; they act not to create a new world, but to open hearts and ears to the one who sits on the throne and says, "Now I am making the whole of creation new" (Rv 21:5).

In our society, which equates worth with productivity, patient action is very difficult. We tend to be so concerned with doing something worthwhile, bringing about changes, planning, organizing, structuring, and restructuring that we often seem to forget that it is not we who redeem, but God. To be busy, "where the action is," and "on top of things" often seem to have become goals themselves. We then have forgotten that our vocation is not to give visibility to our powers but to God's compassion.

Action as the way of a compassionate life is a difficult discipline precisely because we are so in need of recognition and acceptance. This need can easily drive us to conform to the expectation that we will offer something "new." In a society that is so keen on new encounters, so eager for new events, and so hungry for new experiences, it is difficult not to be seduced into impatient activism. Often, we are hardly aware of this seduction, especially since what we are doing is so obviously "good and religious." But even setting up a relief program, feeding the hungry, and assisting the sick could be more an expression of our own needs than of God's call.

But let us not be too moralistic about it: We can never claim pure motives, and it is better to act with and for those who suffer than to wait until we have our own needs completely under control. However, it is important to remain critical of our own activist tendencies. When our own needs begin to dominate our actions, long-range service becomes difficult and we soon become exhausted, burned out, and even embittered by our efforts.

The most important resource for counteracting the constant temptation to slip into activism is the knowledge that in Christ everything has been accomplished. This knowledge should be understood not as an intellectual insight, but as an understanding in faith. As long as we continue to act as if the salvation of the world depends on us, we lack the faith by which mountains can be moved. In Christ, human suffering and pain have already been accepted and suffered; in him our broken humanity has been reconciled and led into the intimacy of the relationship between the Father and the Son. Our action, therefore, must be understood as a discipline by which we make visible what has already been accomplished. Such action is based on the faith that we walk on solid ground even when we are surrounded by chaos, confusion, violence and hatred.

A moving example of this was given by a woman who for many years had lived and worked in Burundi. One day she witnessed a cruel tribal war which destroyed all that she and her co-workers had built up. Many innocent people whom she dearly loved were slaughtered in front of her eyes. Later she was able to say that her knowledge that all this suffering had been accomplished in Christ prevented a mental and emotional breakdown. Her deep understanding of God's saving act enabled her not to leave, but to remain active in the midst of the indescribable misery and to face the real situation with open eyes and open ears. Her actions were not simply an attempt to rebuild and thus to overcome the evils she had seen, but a reminder to her people that God is not a God of hatred and violence but a God of tenderness and compassion. Maybe only those who have suffered much will understand what it means that Christ suffered our pains and accomplished our reconciliation on the cross.

Not Without Confrontation

But activism is not the only temptation that requires discipline. Impatient action not only leads to overworked and overcommitted people but also tends to sentimentalize compassion. Therefore, sentimentality is another temptation for which we need the discipline of action. When we are primarily concerned about being liked, accepted, praised, or rewarded, we become selective in our dos and don'ts. We then tend to limit ourselves to those activities that elicit sympathetic responses. Here we touch on an aspect of compassion that we seldom recognize as such: confrontation. In our society, the discipline of action frequently requires the courage to confront. We are inclined to associate compassion with actions by which wounds are healed and pains relieved. But in a time in which many people can no longer exercise their human rights, millions are hungry, and the whole human race lives under the threat of nuclear holocaust, compassionate action means more than offering help to the suffering. The power of evil has become so blatantly visible in individuals as well as in the social structures that dominate their lives that nothing less than strong and unambiguous confrontation is called for. Compassion does not exclude confrontation. On the contrary, confrontation is an integral part of compassion. The whole prophetic tradition makes this clear, and Jesus is no exception. Sadly enough, Jesus has been presented for so long as a meek and mild person that we seldom realize how differently the Gospels depict him.

In Passolini's film, *The Gospel According to St. Matthew*, we are faced with an aggressive and abrasive prophet who does not avoid irritating people and who at times even seems to invite a negative response. Although Passolini's portrayal of Jesus is one-sided, there is no doubt that he reminds us again of how often Jesus engaged in confrontation and how unconcerned he was about being tactful and pleasing others.

Honest, direct confrontation is a true expression of compassion. As Christians, we are *in* the world without being *of* it. It is precisely this position that renders confrontation both possible and necessary. The illusion of power must be unmasked, idoltry must be undone, oppression and exploitation must be fought, and all who participate in these evils must be confronted. This is compassion. We cannot suffer with the poor when we are unwilling to confront those persons and systems that cause poverty. We cannot set the captives free when we do not want to confront those who carry the keys. We cannot profess our solidarity with those who are oppressed when we are unwilling to confront the oppressor. Compassion without confrontation fades quickly into fruitless sentimental commiseration.

But if confrontation is to be an expression of patient action, it must be humble. Our constant temptation is to fall into self-righteous revenge or self-serving condemnation. The danger here is that our own witness can blind us. When confrontation is tainted by desire for attention, need for revenge, or greed for power, it can easily become self-serving and cease to be compassionate.

It is not easy to confront compassionately. Self-righteousness always lurks around the corner, and violent anger is a real temptation. Probably the best criterion for determining whether our confrontation is compassionate rather than offensive, and our anger righteous rather than self-righteous, is to ask ourselves if we ourselves can be so confronted. Can we learn from indignation directed at us? When we can be confronted by a NO from others, we will be more able to confront a NO. Saying NO to evil and destruction in the awareness that they dwell in our own heart is a humble NO. When we say NO with humility, this NO is also a call for our own conversion. NO to racial injustice means a call to look our own bigotry straight in the eye, and NO to world hunger calls upon us to recognize our own lack of poverty. NO to war requires us to come to terms with our own violence and aggression, and NO to oppression and torture forces us to deal directly with our own insensitivities. And so all our NO's become challenges to purify our own hearts.

In this sense, confrontation always includes self-confrontation. This self-confrontation prevents us from becoming alienated from the world we confront. Thomas Merton saw this clearly when he wrote:

> The world as pure object is something that is not there. It is not a reality outside us for which we exist ... It is a living and self-creating mystery of which I myself am a part, to which I am myself my own unique door. When I find the world in my own ground, it is impossible to be alienated by it.[1]

Here we find the key to compassionate confrontation. The evil that needs to be confronted and fought has an accomplice in the human heart, including our own. Therefore, each attempt to confront evil in the world calls for the realization that there are always two fronts on which the struggle takes place: an outer and an inner front. For confrontation to become and remain compassionate, these fronts should never be separated.

In Gratitude

Whether they confront evil in the world or support the good, disciplined actions are always characterized by gratitude. Anger can make us active and can even unleash in us much creative energy. But not for long. The social activists of the 1960s who allowed their anger to fuel their actions soon found themselves burned out. Often they reached a state of physical as well as mental exhaustion and needed psychotherapy or a "new spirituality." To persevere without visible success we need a spirit of gratitude. An angry action is born of the experience of being hurt; a grateful action is born of the experience of healing. Angry actions want to take; grateful actions want to share. Gratitude is the mark of action undertaken as part of the discipline of patience. It is a response to grace. It leads us not to conquer or destroy, but to give visibility to a good that is already present. Therefore, the compassionate life is a grateful life, and actions born out of gratefulness are not compulsive but free, not somber but joyful, not fanatical but liberating. When gratitude is the source of our actions, our giving becomes receiving, and those to whom we minister become our minsters because in the center of our care for others we sense a caring presence, and in the midst of our efforts we sense an encouraging support. When this happens we can remain joyful and peaceful even when there are few successes to brag about.

A beautiful example of this attitude was demonstrated by Cesar Chavez and his staff when they were defeated after a long campaign for Proposition 14, which tried to secure the right of farmworkers to organize. Instead of a sense of depression, there was a party. Instead of a sense of defeat, there was a sense of victory. A puzzled reporter wrote: "If they celebrate with such joyful festivity when they lose, what will it be like when they win?" What became clear was that Cesar Chavez and the many men and women who had joined him in the campaign for Proposition 14 were so convinced of the righteousness of their actions that the final result became secondary to the value of the action itself. There had been long days of praying and fasting to keep the campaign truthful and honest. There had been hours of singing, scripture reading, and breaking bread together to remind each other that the fruits of all actions come from God. And when finally the action failed and the desired result did not come about, people did not lose hope and courage but simply decided to try again next time. Meanwhile, they had experienced a deep community with each other, had come to know many generous people, and had received a keen sense of God's presence in their midst. They felt that there were reasons to celebrate and be grateful. So no one went home defeated. All had a story to tell, the story of the experience of God's compassion when people gather in his name.

Gratitude is indeed a sign of an action by the discipline of patience. Even when there are no concrete results, the act itself can still be a revelation of God's caring presence here and now. Such action is true action because it is born of true knowledge of God's active presence. It grows not from the need to prove anything or to persuade anyone, but from the desire to give free witness to that which is profoundly real. We find this most powerfully put into words by St. John:

Something which has existed since the beginning,
that we have heard,
that we have seen with our own eyes;
that we have watched
and touched with our hands:
the Word, who is life —
this is our subject.
That life was made visible:
we saw it and we are giving our testimony,
telling you of the eternal life
which was with the Father and has been made visible to us.
What we have seen and heard
we are telling you
so that you too may be in union with us,
as we are in union
with the Father
and with his Son Jesus Christ.
We are writing this to you to make our own joy complete.
(1 Jn 1:1-4)

These words are a most eloquent formulation of the meaning of compassionate action. It is free, joyful, and, above all, grateful manifestation of an encounter that has taken place. The enormous energy with which John, Peter, Paul and all the disciples "conquered" their world with the message of Jesus Christ came from that encounter. They did not have to convince themselves or each other that they were doing a good thing; they had no doubts concerning the value of their work; they had no hesitation about the relevance of their action. They could do nothing other than speak about him, praise him, thank him, and worship him because it was he whom they had heard, seen, and touched. They could do nothing other than bring light to the blind, freedom to the captives and liberty to the oppressed because there they met him again. They could do nothing other than call people together into a new fellowship because thus he would be in their midst. Since Jesus Christ had become their true life, their true concern, their true compassion, and their true love, living became acting and all of life became an ongoing expression of thanks for God's great gift of himself.

This is the deepest meaning of compassionate action. It is the grateful, free and joyful expression of the great encounter with the compassionate God. And it will be fruitful even when we can see neither how nor why. In and through such action, we realize that indeed all is grace and that our only possible response is gratitude.

Footnotes:

1. Merton, Thomas. *Contemplation in a World of Action* (Garden City: Doubleday Image Books, 1971), pp. 154-55.

Ego and Spiritual Materialism

Chögyam Trungpa

Chögyam Trungpa was forced to leave his native Tibet when China invaded it and installed a Communist government there. He has established several centers for Buddhist study and meditation in the British Isles and in the United States, including Naropa Institute, in Boulder, Colorado. Naropa has been the scene of important Buddhist/Christian conferences. In this selection Trungpa deals with ego in spirituality, a problem which is subtle and pervasive.

The approach presented here is a classical Buddhist one — not in a formal sense, but in the sense of presenting the heart of the Buddhist approach to spirituality. Although the Buddhist way is not theistic, it does not contradict the theistic disciplines. Rather the differences between the ways are a matter of emphasis and method. The basic problems of spiritual materialism are common to all spiritual disciplines. The Buddhist approach begins with our confusion and suffering and works toward the unraveling of the origin. The theistic approach begins with the richness of God and works toward raising consciousness so as to experience God's presence. But since the obstacles to relating with God are our confusions and negativities, the theistic approach must also deal with them. Spiritual pride, for example, is as much a problem in theistic disciplines as in Buddhism.

According to the Buddhist tradition, the spiritual path is the process of cutting through our confusion, of uncovering the awakened state of mind. When the awakened state of mind is crowded in by ego and its attendant paranoia, it takes on the character of an underlying instinct. So it is not a matter of building up the awakened state of mind, but rather of burning out the confusions which obstruct it. In the process of burning out the confusions, we discover enlightenment. If the process were otherwise, the awakened state of mind would be a product, dependent upon cause and effect and therefore liable to dissolution. Anything which is created must, sooner or later, die. If enlightenment were created in such a way, there would always be the possibility of ego reasserting itself, causing a return to the confused state. Enlightenment is permanent because we have not produced it; we have merely discovered it. In the Buddhist tradition the analogy of the sun appearing from behind the clouds is often used to explain the discovery of enlightenment. In meditation practice we clear away the confusion of ego in order to glimpse the awakened state. The absence of ignorance, of being crowded in, of paranoia, opens up a tremendous view of life. One discovers a different way of being.

The heart of the confusion is that man has a sense of self which seems to him to be continuous and solid. When a thought or emotion or event occurs, there is a sense of someone being conscious of what is happening. You sense that *you* are reading these words. This sense of self is actually a transitory, discontinuous event, which in our confusion seems to be quite solid and continuous. Since we take our confused view as being real, we struggle to maintain and enhance this solid self. We try to feed it pleasures and shield it from pain. Experience continually threatens to reveal our transitoriness to us, so we continually struggle to cover up any possibility of discovering our real condition. "But," we might ask, "if our real condition is an awakened state, why are we so busy trying to avoid becoming aware of it?" It is because we have become so absorbed in our confused view of the world, that we consider it real, the only possible world. This struggle to maintain the sense of a solid, continuous self is the action of ego.

Ego, however, is only partially successful in shielding us from pain. It is the dissatisfaction which accompanies ego's struggle that inspires us to examine what we are doing. Since there are always gaps in our self-consciousness, some insight is possible.

An interesting metaphor used in Tibetan Buddhism to describe the functioning of ego is that of the "Three Lords of Materialism:" the "Lord of Form," the "Lord of Speech" and the "Lord of Mind." In the discussion of the Three Lords which follows, the words "materialism" and "neurotic" refer to the action of ego.

The Lord of Form refers to the neurotic pursuit of physical comfort, security and pleasure. Our highly organized and technological society reflects our preoccupation with manipulating physical surroundings so as to shield ourselves from the irritations of the raw, rugged, unpredictable aspects of life. Push-button elevators, prepackaged meats, air conditioning, flush toilets, private funerals, retirement programs, mass production, weather satellites, bulldozers, fluorescent lighting, nine-to-five jobs, television — all are attempts to create a manageable, safe, predictable, pleasurable world.

The Lord of Form does not signify the physically rich and secure life-situations we create *per se*. Rather it refers to the neurotic preoccupation that drives us to create them, to try to control nature. It is ego's ambition to secure and entertain itself, trying to avoid all irritation. So we cling to our pleasures and possessions, we fear change or force change, we try to create a nest or playground.

The Lord of Speech refers to the use of intellect in relating to our world. We adopt sets of categories which serve as handles, as ways of managing phenomena. The most fully developed products of this tendency are ideologies, the systems of idea that rationalize, justify and sanctify our lives. Nationalism, communism, existentialism, Christianity, Buddhism — all provide us with identities, rules of action, and interpretations of how and why things happen as they do.

Again, the use of intellect is not in itself the Lord of Speech. The Lord of Speech refers to the inclination on the part of ego to interpret anything that is threatening or irritating in such a way as to neutralize the threat or turn it into something "positive" from ego's point of view. The Lord of Speech refers to the use of concepts as filters to screen us from a direct perception of what is. The concepts are taken too seriously; they are used as tools to solidify our world and ourselves. If a world of nameable things exists, then "I" as one of the nameable things exists as well. We wish not to leave any room for threatening doubt, uncertainity or confusion.

The Lord of Mind refers to the effort of consciousness to maintain awareness of itself. The Lord of Mind rules when we use spiritual and psychological disciplines as the means of maintaining our self-consciousness, of holding onto our sense of self. Drugs, yoga, prayer, meditation, trances, various psychotherapies — all can be used in this way.

Ego is able to convert everything to its own use, even spirituality. For example, if you have learned of a particularly beneficial meditation technique of spiritual practice, then ego's attitude is, first to regard it as an object of fascination and, second to examine it. Finally, since ego is seeming solid and cannot really absorb anything, it can only mimic. Thus ego tries to examine and imitate the practice of meditation and the meditative way of life. When we have learned all the tricks and answers of the spiritual game, we automatically try to imitate spirituality, since real involvement would require the complete elimination of ego, and actually the last thing we want to do is to give up the ego completely. However, we cannot experience that which we are trying to imitate; we can only find some area within the bounds of ego that seems to be the same thing. Ego translates everything in terms of its own state of health, its own inherent qualities. It feels a sense of great accomplishment and excitement at having been able to create such a pattern. At last it has created a tangible accomplishment, a confirmation of its own individuality.

If we become successful at maintaining our self-consciousness through spiritual techniques, then genuine spiritual development is highly unlikely. Our mental habits become so strong as to be hard to penetrate. We may even go so far as to achieve the totally demonic state of complete "Egohood."

Even though the Lord of Mind is the most powerful in subverting spirituality, still the other two Lords can also rule the spiritual practice. Retreat to nature, isolation, simple, quiet, high people — all can be ways of shielding oneself from irritation, all can be expressions of the Lord of Form. Or perhaps religion may provide us with a rationalization for creating a secure nest, a simple but comfortable home, for acquiring an amiable mate, and a stable, easy job.

The Lord of Speech is involved in spiritual practice as well. In following a spiritual path we may substitute a new religious ideology for our former beliefs, but continue to use it in the old neurotic way. Regardless of how sublime our ideas may be, if we take them too seriously and use them to maintain our ego, we are still being ruled by the Lord of Speech.

Most of us, if we examine our actions, would probably agree that we are ruled by one or more of the Three Lords. "But," we might ask, "so what? This is simply a description of the human condition. Yes, we know that our technology cannot shield us from war, crime, illness, economic insecurity, laborious work, old age and death; nor can our ideologies shield us from doubt, uncertainty, confusion and disorientation; nor can our therapies protect us from the dissolution of the high states of consciousness that we may temporarily achieve and the disillusionment and anguish that follow. But what else are we to do? The Three Lords seem too powerful to overthrow, and we don't know what to replace them with."

The Buddha, troubled by these questions, examined the process by which the Three Lords rule. He questioned why our minds follow them and whether there is another way. He discovered that the Three Lords seduce us by creating a fundamental myth: that we are solid beings. But ultimately the myth is false, a huge hoax, a gigantic fraud, and it is the root of our suffering. In order to make this discovery he had to break through very elaborate defenses erected by the Three Lords to prevent their subjects from discovering the fundamental deception which is the source of their power. We cannot in any way free ourselves from the domination of the Three Lords unless we too cut through, layer by layer, the elaborate defenses of these Lords.

The Lords' defenses are created out of the material of our minds. This material of mind is used by the Lords in such a way as to maintain the basic myth of solidity. In order to see for ourselves how this process works we must examine our own experience. "But how," we might ask, "are we to conduct the examination? What method or tool are we to use?" The method that the Buddha discovered is meditation. He discovered that struggling to find answers did not work. It was only when there were gaps in his struggle that insights came to him. He began to realize that there was a sane, awake quality within him which manifested itself only in the absence of struggle. So the practice of meditation involves "letting be."

There have been a number of misconceptions regarding meditation. Some people regard it as a trancelike state of mind. Others think of it in terms of training, in the sense of mental gymnastics. But meditation is neither of these, although it does involve dealing with neurotic states of mind. The neurotic state of mind is not difficult or impossible to deal with. It has energy, speed and a certain pattern. The practice of meditation involves *letting be* — trying to go with the pattern, trying to go with the energy and the speed. In this way we learn how to deal with these factors, how to relate with them, not in the sense of causing them to mature in the way we would like, but in the sense of knowing them for what they are and working with their pattern.

There is a story regarding the Buddha which recounts how he once gave teaching to a famous sitar player who wanted to study meditation. The musician asked, "Should I control my mind or should I completely let go?" The Buddha answered, "Since you are a great musician, tell me how you would tune the strings of your instrument." The musician said, "I would make them not too tight and not too loose." "Likewise," said the Buddha, "in your meditation practice you should not impose anything too forcefully on your mind, nor should you let it wander." That is the teaching of letting the mind *be* in a very open way, of feeling the flow of energy without trying to subdue it and without letting it get out of control, or going with the energy pattern of mind. This is meditation practice.

Such practice is necessary generally because our thinking pattern, our conceptualized way of conducting our life in the world, is either too manipulative, imposing itself upon the world, or else runs completely wild and uncontrolled. Therefore, our meditation practice must begin with ego's outermost layer, the discursive thoughts which continually run through our minds, our mental gossip. The Lords use discursive thought as their first line of defense, as the pawns in their efforts to deceive us. The more we generate thoughts, the busier we are mentally and the more convinced we are of our existence. So the Lords are constantly trying to activate these thoughts, trying to create a constant overlapping of thoughts so that nothing can be seen beyond them. In true meditation there is no ambition to stir up thoughts, nor is there an ambition to suppress them. They are just allowed to occur spontaneously and become an expression of basic sanity. They become the expression of the precision and the clarity of the awakened state of mind.

If the strategy of continually creating overlapping thoughts is penetrated, then the Lords stir up emotions to distract us. The exciting, colorful, dramatic quality of the emotions captures our attention as if we were watching an absorbing film show. In the practice of meditation we neither encourage emotions nor repress them. By seeing them clearly, by allowing them to be as they are, we no longer permit them to serve as a means of entertaining and distracting us. Thus they become the inexhaustible energy which fulfills egoless action.

In the absence of thoughts and emotions the Lords bring up a still more powerful weapon, concepts. Labeling phenomena creates a feeling of a solid definite world of "things." Such a solid world reassures us that we are a solid, continuous thing as well. The world exists, therefore I, the perceiver of the world, exist. Meditation involves seeing the transparency of concepts, so that labeling no longer serves as a way of solidifying our world and our image of self. Labeling becomes simply the act of discrimination. The Lords have still further defense mechanisms, but it would be too complicated to discuss them in this context.

By the examination of his own thoughts, emotions, concepts and the other activities of mind, the Buddha discovered that there is no need to struggle to prove our existence, that we need not be subject to the rule of the Three Lords of Materialism. There is no need to struggle to be free; the absence of struggle is in itself freedom. This egoless state is the attainment of Buddhahood. The process of transforming the material of mind from expressions of ego's ambition into expressions of basic sanity and enlightenment through the practice of meditation — this might be said to be the true spiritual path.

The New Consciousness

Thomas Merton

Thomas Merton, a Cistercian monk of the Abbey of Gethsemane, influenced a great many Christians and non-Christians; the course of his life was probably as influential as anything he wrote. His many books include The Seven Storey Mountain, The Geography of Lograire, The Way of Chuang Tzu, The Wisdom of the Desert, Raids on the Unspeakable, *and* Zen and the Birds of Appetite. *This selection from the latter book shows the way in which Merton was able to use Eastern thought to illuminate aspects of his own Western tradition. Merton died in 1968 in Thailand, at a conference of Buddhist and Christian monks.*

One would like to open this discussion with a reassuring and simple declaration, to say without ambiguity or hesitation: Christian renewal has meant that Christians are now wide open to Asian religions, ready, in the words of Vatican II, to "acknowledge, preserve and promote the spiritual and moral gods" found among them. It is not that simple.

In some respects, progressive Christians were never *less* disposed to this kind of openness. True, they approve all forms of communications and inter-religious dialogue on principle. But the new, secular, "post-Christian" Christianity, which is activistic, antimystical, social and revolutionary, tends to take for granted a great deal of the Marxist assumptions about religion as the opium of the people. In fact, these movements aspire to a kind of Christian repentance on this point, and seek with the greatest fervor to prove that there is no opium about *us*! But, knowing little or nothing about Asian religions, and associating Asia with opium anyway (conveniently forgetting that it was the West that forced opium into China by means of war!), they are still satisfied with the old cliches about "life-denying Buddhism," "selfish navel-gazing," and *Nirvana* as a sort of drugged trance.

The purpose of the present book is not apologetic; but if it were, I should feel myself obliged to argue in favor of Buddhism against these absurd and unexamined prejudices. I might want to suggest, for instance, that a religion which forbids the taking of *any* life without absolute necessity is hardly "life-denying," and to add that it is a little odd that this accusation should be made by people who, some of them invoking the name of Christ, are ravaging a small Asian country with napalm and dynamite, and doing their best to reduce whole areas of the country to a state of lifelessness. But, I repeat, this is not a book of apologetics.

Of course there are many Christians who are very much aware that there is something to be learnt from Hinduism, Buddhism, Confucianism, and especially from Yoga and Zen. Among these are those few Western Jesuits in Japan who have had the courage to practice Zen in Zen monasteries, as well as the Japanese Cistercians who are becoming interested in Zen in their own monasteries. There are also American and European Benedictines who are taking a more than academic interest in Asian religion.

However, there are problems. Both conservative and progressive Christians tend to be suspicious of Asian religion for various reasons. Conservatives because they think all Asian religious thought is pantheistic and imcompatabile with the Christian belief in God as Creator. Progressives because they think all Asian religions are purely and simply world-denying evasions into trance, and systematic repudiations of matter, the body, the senses and so on, with the eventual result that they are passive, quietistic and stagnant. This is part of the general Western myth about the mysterious Orient which is thought to have long since subsided quietly into psychic death, with no hope of any kind of salvation except from the dynamic, creative, life-affirming, progressive West.

Now it is true that the civilizations of India and China — and of other parts of Asia — found it impossible to cope with Western colonialism except by resorting to some of the West's own methods. And it is true that the whole world is in the middle of a cultural and social revolution, the most active center of which is now Asia. Finally, the Chinese cultural revolution is itself one of the most radical, most brutal repudiations of the ancient spiritual heritage of Asia. All these well-known facts give added weight to the prevalent

Western ideas about "Asian mysticism" being at best a kind of systematic moral and intellectual suicide.

The somewhat disconcerting vogue for exploring Asian religious experience in the West does not convince progressive Christians that there is much to it. Beats, hippies and other such types may gain a kind of grudging respect from Christians as quasi-eschatological sects — but their mystical leanings are not what the progressive Christian admires in them. The influence of Barth and the New Orthodoxy (in Protestantism), together with the Biblical renewal everywhere, is probably still very important in this anti-mystical bias.

At the same time, it is not easy to generalize. A "Death-of-God" theologian like Altizer is not only well-informed about Buddhism but also seems to have something of an attraction to it.

Hence nothing too definite can be said about the attitude of the new Christian thinkers toward Hinduism, Buddhism, or Zen — the latter being considered perhaps an "extreme" form of Asian world-denial. The generalized attitude of suspiciousness and negation is based more on ignorance.

This essay will concern itself less with Zen than with the Christian consciousness itself, and with the new development that makes Christianity today frankly activistic, secular and antimystical. Is this new consciousness really a return to a primitive Christian spirit? How does it differ from the kind of consciousness that remained more or less the same from Augustine to Maritain in Western Catholicism?

It was assumed until quite recently that the experience of the first Christians was still accessible to fervent Christians of our day in all its purity, provided certain conditions were faithfully fulfilled. The consciousness of the modern Christian was thought to be essentially the same as that of the Christian of the Apostolic age. If it differed, it did so only in certain accidentals of culture, due to the expansion of the Church in time and space.

Modern scholarship has thoroughly questioned this assumption. It has raised the problem of a radical discontinuity between the experience of the first Christians and that of later generations. The first Christians experienced themselves as men "of the last days," newly created in Christ as members of his new kingdom, expecting his imminent return: they were men entirely delivered from the "old aeon" and from all its concerns. They experienced a new life of liberation "in the Spirit" and the perfect freedom of men who received all from God as pure gift, in Christ, with no further responsibility to "this world" than to announce the glad tidings of the imminent "reestablishment of all things in Christ." They were, in a word, prepared for entry into the kingdom and the new creation in their own lifetime. "Let grace come," said the *Didache*, "and let this world pass away!"

Of course these elements remained present in Christian theology. But the development of a new historical dimension of Christianity radically altered the perspective and consequently also the experience in which these truths of faith were apprehended by Christians as individuals and as a community. With the help of concepts from Hellenic philosophy, these eschatological ideas were given a *metaphysical* dimension. These truths of Christian belief were now experienced "statically" instead of "dynamically," and furthermore, from being intuited metaphysically they also developed into *mystical* experiences.

When it was discovered that the *Parousia* (coming of Christ) was put off into the future, then martyrdom was regarded as the way to enter directly into his kingdom here and now. The experience of martyrdom was in fact, for many of the martyrs, also a mystical experience of union with Christ in his crucifixion and resurrection (see for instance St. Ignatius of Antioch). After the age of the martyrs the ascetics and monks sought union with God in their lives of solitude and self-denial, which they also justified philosophically and theologically by recourse to Hellenic and Oriental ideas. Thus, it is argued, the existential sense of Christian encounter with God in Christ and in the Church as a *happening* (marked by divine freedom and pure gift) became more and more an experience of stabilized *being:* the Christian consciousness was not centered on an event but on the acquisition of a new ontological status and a "new nature." Grace came to be experienced not as God's act but as God's nature shared by "divine sonship" and ultimately in "divinization." This developed eventually into the idea of mystical nuptials with Christ or, in the terms of ontological mysticism (*Wesensmystik*), into absorption in the Godhead through the Word by the action of the Spirit.

There is no space here to develop this critical historical analysis or to evaluate it. What matters is the question it raises: the question of a radical shift in the Christian consciousness, and hence in the Christian's experience of himself in relation to Christ and to the Church. This question is being discussed from many viewpoints in Catholic circles since Vatican II. It is implicit in new explorations of the nature of faith, in new studies of ecclesiology and of Christology, in the new liturgy and everywhere. Conservative Catholics find this question of the accepted categories disturbing. Progressives tend to react forcefully against a metaphysical or even mystical consciousness as "un-Christian."

The metaphysical stability of this ancient view, which over the centuries became traditional, was comforting and secure. Moreover it was inseparable from a stable and authoritarian concept of hierarchical Church structure. A return to a more dynamic and charismatic Christianity — claimed to be that of the first Christians — characterized the Protestant attack on these ancient structures, which depended on a static and metaphysical outlook. More radical Catholics realize this today and perhaps take a certain pleasure is using a fluid, elusive terminology calculated to produce a maximum of anxiety and confusion in less adventurous minds. This dynamism questions all that is static and accepted, and it occasionally makes for good newspaper copy, but the results are not always to be taken very seriously. However that may be, the whole question of Christian, especially Catholic, mysticism is affected by it. If mysticism is summarily identified with the "Hellenic" and "Medieval" Christian experience, it is more and more rejected as non-Christian. The new, radical Catholicism tends to make this identification. The Christian is invited to repudiate all aspiration to personal contemplative union with God and to deep mystical experience, because this is an infidelity to the true Christian revelation, a human substitution for God's saving word, a pagan evasion, an individualistic escape from community. By this token also the Christian dialogue with Oriental religions, with Hinduism and especially with Zen, is considered rather suspect, though of course since dialogue is "progressive" one must not attack it openly as such.

It may however be pertinent to remark here that the term "ecumenism" is not held to be applicable to dialogue with non-Christians. There is an essential difference, say these progressive Catholics, between the dialogue of Catholics with other Christians and the dialogue of Catholics with Hindus or Buddhists. While it is assumed that Catholics and Protestants can learn from each other, and that they can progress together toward a new Christian self-understanding, many progressive Catholics would not concede this to dialogue with non-Christians. Once again, the assumption is that since Hinduism and Buddhism are "metaphysical" and "static" or even "mystical" they have ceased to have any relevance in our time. Only the Catholics who are still convinced of the importance of Christian mysticism are also aware that much is to be learned from a study of the techniques and experience of Oriental religions. But these Catholics are regarded at times with suspicion, if not derision, by progressives and conservatives alike.

The question arises: which outlook comes closer to the primitive Christian experience? Is the supposedly "static" and metaphysical outlook really a rupture and a contradiction, violating the purity of the original Christian awareness? Is the "dynamic" and "existential" approach a return to the primitive view? Must we choose between them?

Is the long tradition of Christian mysticism, from the post-Apostolic age, the Alexandrian and Cappadocian Fathers, down to Eckhart, Tauler, the Spanish mystics and the modern mystics, simply a deviation? When people who cannot entrust themselves to the Church as she now is, nevertheless look with interest and sympathy into the writings of the mystics, are they to be reproved by Christians and admonished to seek rather a more limited and more communal experience of fellowship with progressive believers on the latter's terms? Is this the only true way to understand Christian experience? Is there really a problem, and if there is, what precisely is it? Supposing that the only authentic Christian experience is that of the first Christians, can this be recovered and reconstructed in any way whatever? And if so, is it to be "mystical" or "prophetic"? And in any case, *what is it?* The present notes cannot hope to answer such questions. Their only purpose is to consider the conflict in Christian consciousness today and to make a guess or two that might point toward avenues of further exploration.

First of all, the "Christian consciousness" of modern man can never purely and simply be the consciousness of a first-century inhabitant of the Roman Empire. It is bound to be a modern consciousness.

In our evaluation of the modern consciousness, we have to take into account the still overwhelming importance of the Cartesian *cogito.* Modern man, in so far as he is still Cartesian (he is of course going far beyond Descartes in many respects), is a subject for whom his own self-awareness as a thinking, observing, measuring and estimating "self" is absolutely primary. It is for him the one indubitable "reality," and all truth starts here. The more he is able to develop his consciousness as a subject over against objects, the more he can understand things in their relations to him and one another, the more he can manipulate these objects for his own interests, but also, at the same time, the more he tends to isolate himself in his own subjective prison, to become a detached observer cut off from everything else in a kind of impenetrable alienated and transparent bubble which contains all reality in the form of purely subjective experience. Modern consciousness then tends to create this solipsistic bubble of awareness — an ego-self imprisoned in its own consciousness, isolated and out of touch with other such selves in so far as they are all "things" rather than persons.

It is this kind of consciousness, exacerbated to an extreme, which has made inevitable the so called "death of God." Cartesian thought began with an attempt to reach God as object by starting from the thinking self. But when God becomes object, he sooner or later "dies," because God as object is ultimately unthinkable. God as object is not only a mere abstract concept, but one which contains so many internal contradictions that it becomes entirely nonnegotiable except when it is hardened into an idol that is maintained in existence by a sheer act of will. For a long time man continued to be capable of this willfullness: but now the effort has become exhausting and many Christians have realized it to be futile. Relaxing the effort, they have let go the "God-object" which their fathers and grandfathers still hoped to manipulate for their own ends. Their weariness has accounted for the element of resentment which made this a conscious "murder" of the deity. Liberated from the strain of wilfully maintaining an object-God in existence, the Cartesian consciousness remains none the less imprisoned in itself. Hence the need to break out of itself and to meet "the other" in "encounter," "openness," "fellowship," "communion."

Yet the great problem is that for the Cartesian consciousness the "other," too, is object. There is no need here to retail the all-important modern effort to restore man's awareness of his fellow man to an "I-Thou" status. Is a genuine I-Thou relationship possible *at all* to a purely Cartesian subject?

Meanwhile, let us remind ourselves that another, metaphysical, consciousness is still available to modern man. It starts not from the thinking and self-aware subject but from Being, ontologically seen to be beyond and prior to the subject-object division. Underlying the subjective experience of the individual self there is an immediate experience of Being. This is totally different from an experience of self-consciousness. It is completely nonobjective. It has in it none of the split and alienation that occurs when the subject becomes aware of itself as a quasi-object. The consciousness of Being (whether considered positively or negatively and apophatically as in Buddhism) is an immediate experience that goes beyond reflexive awareness. It is not "consciousness *of*" but *pure consciousness*, in which the subject as such "disappears."

Posterior to this immediate experience of a ground which transcends experience, emerges the subject with its self-awareness. But, as the Oriental religions and Christian mysticism have stressed, this self-aware subject is not final or absolute; it is a provisional self-construction which exists, for practical purposes, only in a sphere of relativity. Its existence has meaning in so far as it does not become fixated or centered upon itself as ultimate, learns to function not as its own center but "from God" and "for others." The Christian term "from God" implies what the nontheistic religious philosophies conceive as a hypothetical Single Center of all beings, what T. S. Eliot called "the still point of the turning world," but which Buddhism for example visualizes not as "point" but as "Void." (And of course the Void is not visualized at all.)

In brief, this form of consciousness assumes a totally different kind of self-awareness from that of the Cartesian thinking-self which is its own justification and its own center. Here the individual is aware of himself as a self-to-be-dissolved in self-giving, in love, in "letting-go," in ecstasy, in God — there are many ways of phrasing it.

The self is not its own center and does not orbit around itself; it is centered on God, the one center of all, which is "everywhere and nowhere," in whom all are encountered, from whom all proceed. Thus from the very start this consciousness is disposed to encounter "the other" with whom it is already united anyway "in God."

The metaphysical intuition of Being is an intuition of a *ground of openness*, indeed of a kind of ontological openness and an infinite generosity which communicates itself to everything that is. "The good is diffusive of itself," or "God is love." Openness is not something to be acquired, but a radical gift that has been lost and must be recovered (though it is still in principle "there" in the roots of our created being). This is more or less metaphysical language, but there is also a non-metaphysical way of stating this. It does not consider God either as Immanent or as Transcendent but as grace and presence, hence neither as a "Center" imagined somewhere "out there" nor "within ourselves." It encounters him not as Being but as Freedom and Love. I would say from the outset that the important thing is not to *oppose* this gracious and prophetic concept to the metaphysical and mystical idea of union with God, but to show where the two ideas really seek to express the same kind of consciousness or at least to approach it, in varying ways.

The Love of God and Affliction[1]

Simone Weil

Simone Weil died in England in 1943, where she had gone to work with the French Provisional government. Although she became a firm believer in Catholicism, Weil felt that it was her vocation to remain outside the Catholic Church and was never baptized. Her influence on Christians of every denomination has been profound. The severe and demanding quality of mind which is revealed in her writing was revealed in her life as well: she lived in extreme simplicity, and died because despite illness she refused to eat more than the rations to which her French compatriots were limited.

In the realm of suffering, affliction is something apart, specific, and irreducible. It is quite a different thing from simple suffering. It takes possession of the soul and marks it through and through with its own particular mark, the mark of slavery. Slavery as practiced by ancient Rome is only an extreme form of affliction. The men of antiquity, who knew all about this question, used to say: "A man loses half his soul the day he becomes a slave."

Affliction is inseparable from physical suffering and yet quite distinct. With suffering, all that is not bound up with physical pain or something analogous is artificial, imaginary, and can be eliminated by a suitable adjustment of the mind. Even in the case of the absence or death of someone we love, the irreducible part of the sorrow is akin to physical pain, a difficulty in breathing, a constriction of the heart, an unsatisfied need, hunger, or the almost biological disorder caused by the brutal liberation of some energy, hitherto directed by an attachment and now left without a guide. A sorrow that is not centered around an irreducible core of such a nature is mere romanticism or literature. Humiliation is also a violent condition of the whole corporal being, which longs to surge up under the outrage but is forced by impotence or fear, to hold itself in check.

On the other hand pain that is only physical is a very unimportant matter and leaves no trace in the soul. Toothache is an example. An hour of two of violent pain caused by a decayed tooth is nothing once it is over.

It is another matter if the physical suffering is very prolonged or frequent, but in such a case we are dealing with something quite different from an attack of pain; it is often an affliction.

Affliction is an uprooting of life, a more or less attenuated equivalent of death, made irresistibly present to the soul by the attack or immediate apprehension of physical pain. If there is complete absence of physical pain there is no affliction for the soul, because our thoughts can turn to any object. Thought flies from affliction as promptly and irresistibly as an animal flies from death. Here below, physical pain, and that alone, has the power to chain down our thoughts; on condition that we count as physical pain certain phenomena that, though difficult to describe, are bodily and exactly equivalent to it. Fear of physical pain is a notable example.

When thought is obliged by an attack of physical pain, however slight, to recognize the presence of affliction, a state of mind is brought about, as acute as that of a condemned man who is forced to look for hours at the guillotine that is going to cut off his head. Human beings can live for twenty or fifty years in this acute state. We pass quite close to them without realizing it. What man is capable of discerning such souls unless Christ himself looks through his eyes? We only notice that they have rather a strange way of behaving and we censure this behavior.

There is not real affliction unless the event that has seized and uprooted a life attacks it, directly or indirectly, in all its parts, social, psychological, and physical. The social factor is essential. There is not really affliction unless there is social degradation or the fear of it in some form or another.

There is both continuity and the separation of a definite point of entry, as with the temperature at which water boils, between affliction itself and all the sorrows that, even though they may be very violent, very deep and very lasting, are not affliction in the strict sense. There is a limit; on the far side of it we have affliction but not on the near side. This limit is not purely objective; all sorts of personal factors have to be taken into account. The same event may plunge one human being into affliction and not another.

The great enigma of human life is not suffering but affliction. It is not surprising that the innocent are killed, tortured, driven from their country, made destitute, or reduced to slavery, imprisoned in camps or cells, since there are criminals to perform such actions. It is not surprising either that disease is the cause of long sufferings, which paralyze life and make it into an image of death, since nature is at the mercy of the blind play of mechanical necessities. But it *is* surprising that God should have given affliction the power to seize the very souls of the innocent and to take possession of them as their sovereign lord. At the very best, he who is branded by affliction will keep only half his soul.

As for those who have been struck by one of those blows that leave a being struggling on the ground like a half-crushed worm, they have no words to express what is happening to them. Among the people they meet, those who have never had contact with affliction in its true sense can have no idea of what it is, even though they may have suffered a great deal. Affliction is something specific and impossible to describe in any other terms, as sounds are to anyone who is deaf and dumb. And as for those who have themselves been mutilated by affliction, they are in no state to help anyone at all, and they are almost incapable of even wishing to do so. Thus compassion for the afflicted is an impossibility. When it is really found we have a more astounding miracle than walking on water, healing the sick, or even raising the dead.

Affliction constrained Christ to implore that he might be spared, to seek consolation from man, to believe he was forsaken by the Father. It forced a just man to cry out against God, a just man as perfect as human nature can be, more so, perhaps, if Job is less a historical character than a figure of Christ. "He laughs at the affliction of the innocent!" This is not a blasphemy but a genuine cry of anguish. The Book of Job is a pure marvel of truth and authenticity from beginning to end. As regards affliction, all that departs from this model is more or less stained with falsehood.

Affliction makes God appear to be absent for a time, more absent than a dead man, more absent than light in the utter darkness of a cell. A kind of horror submerges the whole soul. During this absence there is nothing to love. What is terrible is that if, in this darkness where there is nothing to love, the soul ceases to love, God's absence becomes final. The soul has to go on loving in the emptiness, or at least to go on wanting to love, though it may only be with an infinitesimal part of itself. Then, one day, God will come to show himself to this soul and to reveal the beauty of the world to it, as in the case of Job. But if the soul stops loving it falls, even in this life, into something almost equivalent to hell.

That is why those who plunge men into affliction before they are prepared to receive it kill their souls. On the other hand, in a time such as ours, where affliction is hanging over us all, help given to souls is effective only if it goes far enough really to prepare them for affliction. That is no small thing.

Affliction hardens and discourages us because, like a red hot iron, it stamps the soul to its very depths with the scorn, the disgust, and even the self-hatred and sense of guilt and defilement that crime logically should produce but actually does not. Evil dwells in the heart of the criminal without being felt there. It is felt in the heart of the man who is afflicted and innocent. Everything happens as though the state of soul suitable for criminals had been separated from crime and attached to affliction; and it even seems to be in proportion to the innocence of those who are afflicted.

If Job cries out that he is innocent in such despairing accents, it is because he himself is beginning not to believe in it; it is because his soul within him is taking the side of his friends. He implores God himself to bear witness, because he no longer hears the testimony of his own conscience; it is no longer anything but an abstract, lifeless memory for him.

Men have the same carnal nature as animals. If a hen is hurt, the others rush upon it, attacking it with their beaks. This phenomenon is as automatic as gravitation. Our senses attach all the scorn, all the revulsion, all the hatred that our reason attaches to crime, to affliction. Except for those whose whole soul is inhabited by Christ, everybody despises the afflicted to some extent, although practically no one is conscious of it.

This law of sensibility also holds good with regard to ourselves. In the case of someone in affliction, all the scorn, revulsion, and hatred are turned inward. They penetrate to the center of the soul and from there color the whole universe with their poisoned light. Supernatural love, if it has survived, can prevent this second result from coming about, but not the first. The first is of the very essence of affliction; there is no affliction without it.

Christ ... being made a curse for us. It was not only the body of Christ, hanging on the wood, that was accursed; it was his whole soul also. In the same way every innocent being in his affliction feels himself accursed. This even goes on being true for those who have been in affliction and have come out of it, through a change in their fortunes, that is to say, if the affliction ate deeply enough into them.

Another effect of affliction is, little by little, to make the soul its accomplice, by injecting a poison of inertia into it. In anyone who has suffered affliction for a long enough time there is a complicity with regard to his own affliction. This complicity impedes all the efforts he might make to improve his lot; it goes so far as to prevent him from seeking a way of deliverance, sometimes even to the point of preventing him from wishing for deliverance. Then he is established in affliction, and people might think he was satisfied. Further, this complicity may even induce him to shun the means of deliverance. In such cases it veils itself with excuses which are often ridiculous. Even a person who has come through his affliction will still have something left in him compelling him to plunge into it again, if it has bitten deeply and forever into the substance of his soul. It is as though affliction had established itself in him like a parasite and were directing him to suit its own purposes. Sometimes this impulse triumphs over all the movements of the soul toward happiness. If the affliction has been ended as a result of some kindness, it may take the form of hatred for the benefactor; such is the cause of certain apparently inexplicable acts of savage ingratitude. It is sometimes easy to deliver an unhappy man from his present distress, but it is difficult to set him free from his past affliction. Only God can do it. And even the grace of God itself cannot cure irremediably wounded nature here below. The glorified body of Christ bore the marks of the nails and spear.

One can only accept the existence of affliction by considering it at a distance.

God created through love and for love. God did not create anything except love itself, and the means to love. He created love in all its forms. He created beings capable of love from all possible distances. Because no other could do it, he himself went to the greatest possible distance, the infinite distance. This infinite distance between God and God, this supreme tearing apart, this agony beyond all others, this marvel of love, is the crucifixion. Nothing can be further from God than that which has been made accursed.

This tearing apart, over which supreme love places the bond of supreme union, echoes perpetually across the universe in the midst of the silence, like two notes, separate yet melting into one, like pure and heart-rending harmony. This is the Word of God. The whole creation is nothing but its vibration. When human music in its greatest purity pierces our soul, this is what we hear through it. When we have learned to hear the silence, this is what we grasp more distinctly through it.

Those who persevere in love hear this note from the very lowest depths into which affliction has thrust them. From that moment they can no longer have any doubt.

Men struck down by affliction are at the foot of the Cross, almost at the greatest possible distance from God. It must not be thought that sin is a greater distance. Sin is not a distance, it is a turning of our gaze in the wrong direction.

It is true that there is a mysterious connection between this distance and an original disobedience. From the beginning, we are told, humanity turned its gaze away from God and walked in the wrong direction for as far as it could go. That was because it could walk then. As for us, we are nailed down to the spot, only free to choose which way we look, ruled by necessity. A blind mechanism, heedless of degrees of spiritual perfection, continually tosses men about and throws some of them at the very foot of the Cross. It rests with them to keep or not to keep their eyes turned toward God through all the jolting. It does not mean that God's Providence is lacking. It is in his Providence that God has willed that necessity should be like a blind mechanism.

If the mechanism were not blind there would not be any affliction. Affliction is anonymous before all things; it deprives its victims of their personality and makes them into things. It is indifferent; and it is the coldness of this indifference — a metallic coldness — that freezes all those it touches right to the depths of their souls. They will never find warmth again. They will never believe any more that they are anyone.

Affliction would not have this power without the element of chance contained by it. Those who are persecuted for their faith and are aware of the fact are not afflicted, although they have to suffer. They only fall into a state of affliction if suffering or fear fills the soul to the point of making it forget the cause of the persecution. The martyrs who entered the arena, singing as they went to face the wild beasts, were not afflicted. Christ was afflicted. He did not die like a martyr. He died like a common criminal, confused with thieves, only a little more ridiculous. For affliction is ridiculous.

Only blind necessity can throw men to the extreme point of distance, right next to the Cross. Human crime, which is the cause of most affliction, is part of blind necessity, because criminals do not know what they are doing.

There are two forms of friendship: meeting and separation. They are indissoluble. Both of them contain some good, and this good of friendship is unique, for when two beings who are not friends are near each other there is no meeting, and when friends are far apart there is no separation. As both forms contain the same good thing, they are both equally good.

God produces himself and knows himself perfectly, just as we in our miserable fashion make and know objects outside ourselves. But, before all things, God is love. Before all things God loves himself. This love, this friendship of God, is the Trinity. Between the terms united by this relation of divine love there is more than nearness; there is infinite nearness or identity. But, resulting from the Creation, the Incarnation, and the Passion, there is also infinite distance. The totality of space and the totality of time, interposing their immensity, put an infinite distance between God and God.

Lovers or friends desire two things. The one is to love each other so much that they enter into each other and only make one being. The other is to love each other so much that, with half the globe between them, their union will not be diminished in the slightest degree. All that man vainly desires here below is perfectly realized in God. We have all those impossible desires within us as a mark of our destination, and they are good for us when we no longer hope to accomplish them.

The love between God and God, which in itself *is* God, is this bond of double virtue: the bond that unites two beings so closely that they are no longer distinguishable and really form a single unity and the bond that stretches across distance and triumphs over infinite separation. The unity of God, wherein all plurality disappears, and the abandonment, wherein Christ believes he is left while never ceasing to love his Father perfectly, these are two forms expressing the divine virtue of the same Love, the Love that is God himself.

God is so essentially love that the unity, which in a sense is his actual definition, is the pure effect of love. Moreover, corresponding to the infinite virtue of unification belonging to this love, there is the infinite separation over which it triumphs, which is the whole creation spread throughout the totality of space and time, made of mechanically harsh matter and interposed between Christ and his Father.

As for us men, our misery gives us the infinitely precious privilege of sharing in this distance placed between the Son and his Father. This distance is only separation, however, for those who love. For those who love, separation, although painful, is a good, because it is love. Even the distress of the abandoned Christ is a good. There cannot be a greater good for us on earth than to share in it. God can never be perfectly present to us here below on account of our flesh. Bu he can be almost perfectly absent from us in extreme affliction. This is the only possibility of perfection for us on earth. That is why the Cross is our only hope. "No forest bears such a tree, with such blossoms, such foliage, and such fruit."

This universe where we are living, and of which we form a tiny particle, is the distance put by Love between God and God. We are a point in this distance. Space, time, and the mechanism that governs matter are the distance. Everything that we call evil is only this mechanism. God has provided that when his grace penetrates to the very center of a man and from there illuminates all his being, he is able to walk on the water without violating any of the laws of nature. When, however, a man turns away from God, he simply gives himself up to the law of gravity. Then he thinks that he can decide and choose, but he is only a thing, a stone that falls. If we examine human society and souls closely and with real attention, we see that wherever the virtue of supernatural light is absent, everything is obedient to mechanical laws as blind and as exact as the laws of gravitation. To know this is profitable and necessary. Those whom we call criminals are only tiles blown off a roof by the wind and falling at random. Their only fault is the initial choice by which they became such tiles.

The mechanism of necessity can be transposed to any level while still remaining true to itself. It is the same in the world of pure matter, in the animal world, among nations, and in souls. Seen from our present standpoint, and in human perspective, it is quite blind. If, however, we transport our hearts beyond ourselves, beyond the universe, beyond space and time to where our Father dwells, and if from there we behold this mechanism, it appears quite different. What seemed to be necessity becomes obedience. Matter is entirely passive and in consequence entirely obedient to God's will. It is a perfect model for us. There cannot be any being other than God and that which obeys God. On account of its perfect obedience, matter deserves to be loved by those who love its Master, in the same ways as a needle, handled by the beloved wife he has lost, is cherished by a lover. The beauty of the world gives us an intimation of its claim to a place in our heart. In the beauty of the world brute necessity becomes an object of love. What is more beautiful than the action of gravity on the fugitive folds of the sea waves, or on the almost eternal folds of the mountains?

The sea is not less beautiful in our eyes because we know that sometimes ships are wrecked by it. On the contrary, this adds to its beauty. If it altered the movement of its waves to spare a boat, it would be a creature gifted with discernment and choice and not this fluid, perfectly obedient to every external pressure. It is this perfect obedience that constitutes the sea's beauty.

All the horrors produced in this world are like the folds imposed upon the waves by gravity. That is why they contain an element of beauty. Sometimes a poem, such as the *Iliad*, brings this beauty to light.

Men can never escape from obedience to God. A creature cannot but obey. The only choice given to men, as intelligent and free creatures, is to desire obedience or not to desire it. If a man does not desire it, he obeys nevertheless, perpetually, inasmuch as he is a thing subject to mechanical necessity. If he desires it, he is still subject to mechanical necessity, but a new necessity is added to it, a necessity constituted by laws belonging to supernatural things. Certain actions become impossible for him; others are done by his agency, sometimes almost in spite of himself.

When we have the feeling that on some occasion we have disobeyed God, it simply means that for a time we have ceased to desire obedience. Of course it must be understood that, where everything else is equal, a man does not perform the same actions if he gives his consent to obedience as if he does not; just as a plant, where everything else is equal, does not grow in the same way in the light as in the dark. The plant does not have any control or choice in the matter of its own growth. As for us, we are like plants that have the one choice of being in or out of the light.

Christ proposed the docility of matter to us as a model when he told us to consider the lilies of the field that neither toil nor spin. This means that they have not set out to clothe themselves in this or that color; they have not exercised their will or made arrangements to bring about their object; they have received all that natural necessity brought them. If they appear to be infinitely more beautiful than the richest stuffs, it is not because they are richer but a result of their docility. Materials are docile too, but docile to man, not to God. Matter is not beautiful when it obeys man, but only when it obeys God. If sometimes a work of art seems almost as beautiful as the sea, the mountains, or flowers, it is because the light of God has filled the artist. In order to find things beautiful which are manufactured by men uninspired by God, it would be necessary for us to have understood with our whole soul that these men themselves are only matter, capable of obedience without knowledge. For anyone who has arrived at this point, absolutely everything here below is perfectly beautiful. In everything that exists, in everything that comes about, he discerns the mechanism of necessity, and he appreciates in necessity the infinite sweetness of obedience. For us, this obedience of things in relation to God is what the transparency of a window pane is in relation to light. As soon as we feel this obedience with our whole being, we see God.

When we hold a newspaper upside down, we see the strange shapes of the printed characters. When we turn it the right way up, we no longer see the characters, we see words. The passenger on board a boat caught in a storm feels each jolt as an inward upheaval. The captain is only aware of the complex combination of the wind, the current, and the swell, with the position of the boat, its shape, its sails, its rudder.

As one has to learn to read or to practice a trade, so one must learn to feel in all things, first and almost solely, the obedience of the universe to God. It is really an apprenticeship. Like every apprenticeship, it requires time and effort. He who has reached the end of his training realizes that the differences between things or between events are no more important than those recognized by someone who knows how to read, when he has before him the same sentence reproduced several times, written in red ink and blue, and printed in this, that, or the other kind of lettering. He who does not know how to read only sees the differences. For him who knows how to read, it all comes to the same thing, since the sentence is identical. Whoever has finished his apprenticeship recognizes things and events, everywhere and always, as vibrations of the same divine and infinitely sweet word. This does not mean that he will not suffer. Pain is the color of certain events. When a man who can and a man who cannot read look at a sentence written in red ink, they both see the same red color, but this color is not so important for the one as for the other.

When an apprentice gets hurt, or complains of being tired, the workmen and peasants have this fine expression: "It is the trade entering his body." Each time that we have some pain to go through, we can say to ourselves quite truly that it is the universe, the order, and beauty of the world and the obedience of creation to God that are entering our body. After that how can we fail to bless with tenderest gratitude the Love that sends us this gift?

Joy and suffering are two equally precious gifts both of which must be savored to the full, each one in its purity, without trying to mix them. Through joy, the beauty of the world penetrates our soul. Through suffering it penetrates our body. We could no more become friends of God through joy alone than one becomes a ship's captain by studying books on navigation. The body plays a part in all apprenticeships. On the plane of physical sensibility, suffering alone gives us contact with that necessity which constitutes the order of the world, for pleasure does not involve an impression of necessity. It is a higher kind of sensibility, capable of recognizing a necessity in joy, and that only indirectly through a sense of beauty. In order that our being should one day become wholly sensitive in every part to this obedience that is the substance of matter, in order that a new sense should be formed in us to enable us to hear the universe as the vibration of the word of God, the transforming power of suffering and of joy are equally indispensable. When either of them comes to us we have to open the very center of our soul to it, just as a woman opens her door to messengers from her loved one. What does it matter to a lover if the messenger be polite or rough, so long as he delivers the message?

But affliction is not suffering. Affliction is something quite distinct from a method of God's teaching.

The infinity of space and time separates us from God. How are we to seek for him? How are we to go toward him? Even if we were to walk for hundreds of years, we should do no more than go round and round the world. Even in an airplane we could not do anything else. We are incapable of progressing vertically. We cannot take a step toward the heavens. God crosses the universe and comes to us.

Over the infinity of space and time, the infinitely more infinite love of God comes to possess us. He comes at his own time. We have the power to consent to receive him or to refuse. If we remain deaf, he comes back again and again like a beggar, but also, like a beggar, one day he stops coming. If we consent, God puts a little seed in us and he goes away again. From that moment God has no more to do; neither have we, except to wait. We only have not to regret the consent we gave him, the nuptial yes. It is not as easy as it seems, for the growth of the seed within us is painful. Moreover, from the very fact that we accept this growth, we cannot avoid destroying whatever gets in its way, pulling up the weeds, cutting the good grass, and unfortunately the good grass is part of our very flesh, so that this gardening amounts to a violent operation. On the whole, however, the seed grows of itself. A day comes when the soul belongs to God, when it not only consents to love but when truly and effectively it loves. Then in its turn it must cross the universe to go to God. The soul does not love like a creature with created love. The love within it is divine, uncreated; for it is the love of God for God that is passing through it. God alone is capable of loving God. We can only consent to give up our own feelings so as to allow free passage in our soul for this love. That is the meaning of denying oneself. We are created for this consent, and for this alone.

Divine Love crossed the infinity of space and time to come from God to us. But how can it repeat the journey in the opposite direction, starting from a finite creature? When the seed of divine love placed in us has grown and become a tree, how can we, we who bear it, take it back to its origin? How can we repeat the journey made by God when he came to us, in the opposite direction? How can we cross infinite distance?

It seems impossible, but there is a way — a way with which we are familiar. We know quite well in what likeness this tree is made, this tree that has grown within us, this most beautiful tree where the birds of the air come and perch. We know what is the most beautiful of all trees. "No forest bears its equal." Something still a little more frightful than a gibbet — that is the most beautiful of all trees. It was the seed of this tree that God placed within us, without our knowing what seed it was. If we had known, we should not have said yes at the first moment. It is this tree that has grown within us and has become ineradicable. Only a betrayal could uproot it.

When we hit a nail with a hammer, the whole of the shock received by the large head of the nail passes into the point without any of it being lost, although it is only a point. If the hammer and the head of the nail were infinitely big it would be just the same. The point of the nail would transmit this infinite shock at the point to which it was applied.

Extreme affliction, which means physical pain, distress of soul, and social degradation, all at the same time, is a nail whose point is applied at the very center of the soul, whose head is all necessity spreading throughout space and time.

Affliction is a marvel of divine technique. It is a simple and ingenious device which introduces into the soul of a finite creature the immensity of force, blind, brutal, and cold. The infinite distance separating God from the creature is entirely concentrated into one point to pierce the soul in its center.

The man to whom such a thing happens has no part in the operation. He struggles like a butterfly pinned alive into an album. But through all the horror he can continue to want to love. There is nothing impossible in that, no obstacle, one might almost say no difficulty. For the greatest suffering, so long as it does not cause the soul to faint, does not touch the acquiescent part of the soul, consenting to a right direction.

It is only necessary to know that love is a direction and not a state of the soul. If one is unaware of this, one falls into despair at the first onslaught of affliction.

He whose soul remains ever turned toward God though the nail pierces it finds himself nailed to the very center of the universe. It is the true center; it is not in the middle; it is beyond space and time; it is God. In a dimension that does not belong to space, that is not time, that is indeed quite a different dimension, this nail has pierced cleanly through all creation, through the thickness of the screen separating the soul from God.

In this marvelous dimension, the soul, without leaving the place and the instant where the body to which it is united is situated, can cross the totality of space and time and come into the very presence of God.

It is at the intersection of creation and its Creator. This point of intersection is the point of intersection of the arms of the Cross.

Saint Paul was perhaps thinking about things of this kind when he said: "That ye, being rooted and grounded in love, may be able to comprehend with all saints what is the breadth, and length, and depth, and height; and to know the love of Christ, which passeth knowledge."[2]

Footnotes:

1. No English word exactly conveys the meaning of the French *malheur*. Our word *unhappiness* is a negative term and far too weak. Affliction is the nearest equivalent but not quite satisfactory. *Malheur* has in it a sense of inevitability and doom.
2. Epistle to the Ephesians 3:17-19.